D0573329

MICHAEL BOLTON

TIME, LOVE, AND TENDERNESS

Lee Randall

A FIRESIDE BOOK

PUBLISHED BY SIMON & SCHUSTER

New York   London   Toronto   Sydney   Tokyo   Singapore

Title page photograph: Bill Thorup/X-Press Studio

FIRESIDE
Simon & Schuster Building
Rockefeller Center
1230 Avenue of the Americas
New York, New York 10020

FIRESIDE and colophon are registered trademarks
of Simon & Schuster Inc.

Designed by Stanley S. Drate, Folio Graphics Co., New York

Produced by March Tenth, Inc.

Manufactured in the United States of America

10   9   8   7   6   5   4   3   2   1

Library of Congress Cataloging-in-Publication Data
is available.

ISBN: 0-671-87304-0

Acknowledgments

Special thanks to Michael Pietsch for his ongoing encouragement and for teaching me not to give it away. Extra-special thanks to David and Janille Randall for their endless love and support (no matter how unlovable and insupportable I get).

Thanks also to the following people, who helped make this possible: Chuck Adams; Christopher Arnott at the *New Haven Advocate*; Susan Carolonza; Celebrity Photo; Cara & Michael; Sandra Choron; Peter Davis; Cindy Dopkin; Brian Douglas; Phil at Duggal; Philip Ehrlich; Mary Flanagan; Virginia Lohle at Star File; Steve Lowry; Dennis Nardella; Charles Neher; Lee at Retna; Mark Ridings; Bill Thorup; Ernst Weber, Jr. (and Mary—you guys are way cool!); and Josleen Wilson.

Contents

Introduction

Like Dorothy in Oz, Michael Bolton always had the power to get what he wanted. He possessed all the requirements for stardom: matinee-idol bone structure, legendary hair, powerful lungs, and a repertoire of heart-wrenching love songs wrapped around hooks that dig under your skin. Today this killer combination sends women into orbit, and that excitement translates into multi-platinum record sales. But there was a time when Bolton narrowly missed crapping out.

This is the story of his sixteen-year struggle and dramatic turnaround from the second string to top of the charts and tops in women's fantasies. It's a story riddled with oppositions. What excites Bolton's fans inflames the critics. The tunes he wrote and gave away solved monetary problems, but they were the very songs he needed to make his name as a performer. And privately, Bolton faced some of his toughest personal tests at the peak of his professional triumphs.

Michael Bolton is the crooner critics love to hate. The louder fans scream "More!" the louder critics bellow "Yuck!" Karen Schoemer, of *The New York Times*, dismissed Bolton as "the Engelbert Humperdink of our day." *Newsday*'s John Leland wrote, "If he were any more middle of the road, he'd have a white line down his forehead . . . [He] sings in a tortured, stone-washed voice that couldn't make a bird jump off a twig."

Harsh reviews have naturally bred some snippiness on Bolton's part, but he's clever enough to know who has the last laugh: "Fortunately, critics don't affect record sales and they don't affect my concerts. . . . Some of these guys shouldn't be allowed to critique music. They don't understand how chemistry is created between a singer and an audience."

Call it chemistry or biology, a key factor of Bolton's success is sex appeal. Roughly 75 to 80 percent of his supporters are women from the ages of fifteen to sixty-five. They inundate his fan club with 1,500 letters each week. The pandemonium at a Bolton concert recalls the heyday of Frank Sinatra, Paul Anka, or the Beatles—women scream and swoon, underwear is jettisoned, flowers blanket the footlights, and the perfume-drenched air fills with catcalls begging Michael to strip down and flash some skin. "Show us your butt!" comes the boldest holler.

It's easy enough to understand why they're delirious. Bolton might have stepped off the cover of a bestselling romance novel. He's a sinuous, six-foot-tall, leggy hunk with a long, blondish mane, sparkling hazel eyes, cheekbones that could slice paper, a dazzling diamond stud earring, and an intense gaze that easily penetrates female hearts. One writer called Bolton a "historical sampling of masculine ideals: forties dreamboat, hair-flipping rock star, Spartan spear-chucker."

Best of all, from a fan's perspective, this gorgeous exterior holds a man with deeply felt emotions that find expression in his songs. In *The New York Times* Charles M. Young noted, "Emotion is what Michael Bolton packs into his ballads, with the promise that here's a guy who'll even (gasp!) share his feelings." Bolton manages to do so without succumbing to "wussiness," like so many others who've given sensitivity a bad name. Testosterone suffuses his vocals, and women respond approvingly.

Women adore Bolton. They clamor for intimate details about this intensely private, compelling man and write letters to magazine editors begging for stories about their hero. Ordinarily such requests remain the private fodder of editorial meetings, but in an unprecedented move, *Vanity Fair* published two pleas in December 1992, commenting, "[We have] received more than a dozen letters of the sort printed below:"

"You seem to be featuring quite a few women on your covers. How about their male counterpart, Michael Bolton? He has his own softball team . . . and there have been rumors of movie offers"—Lynn Lewis, Canton, Michigan.

"What about featuring a favorite of mine, Michael Bolton—singer, songwriter, and great looking guy? He came out first in a most-popular-male-singer poll recently. Even Oprah thinks he's terrific"—Sally Freeman, Colorado Springs, Colorado.

Michael Angeli's incisive profile of Bolton for *Esquire* (in January 1993) reflected a similar phenomenon. His story is peppered with excerpts from reader letters:

"To the Editor: You're missing something special! Michael Bolton deserves an interview—in fact, he deserves a cover! To heck with the critics"—Jean L. George, Tamaqua, Pennsylvania.

"To the Editor of *Esquire*: After Elvis died, I thought I would NEVER get interested in any other singer. I was EXTREMELY surprised when I heard Michael Bolton's VOICE"—Christina Pau-Preto, Milford, Massachusetts.

"Dear Editor: Michael Bolton is The Love of My Life. I'm writing this because I believe Michael would be perfect for your magazine. He looks so good in anything he wears"—Marilyn Borri, Warren, Michigan.

After his appearance as a *People* coverboy in December 1992, fans wrote to thank *and* chastise the magazine. One statistician from Virginia scolded: "Your article was long overdue. It has been exactly two years, seven months and seven days since you last featured this talented performer."

A Minnesota fan wrote: "Watching and listening to him is like watching a good friend who has finally made it to the top." From Florida came the affirmation: "You struck gold. Who cares what the critics think? It's the loyal fans he sings for who matter, and we are so happy for him and the success he has finally achieved."

Sexiness helped turn Bolton into a superstar, but hormones aren't the whole story. Talent and astounding determination are overriding constants in Bolton's rise to fame. Michael Bolton has given his entire life to music. Even as a child he dreamed of expressing himself through song. His current stature comes as a pleasant reward, since it's the culmination of years of hard work. "I take a certain pride in the fact that I've earned it," he says.

What makes Bolton run? How did he endure sixteen years of uphill struggle? Michael Bolton grabbed his dream with pitbull tenacity because he's one competitive guy. With a self-deprecating laugh that masks utter seriousness, Michael explains, "It's not how much I love to win, it's how much I hate to lose."

Nowadays Bolton plays in the majors—and he's on a non-stop winning streak.

GREAT AMERICAN MUSIC HALL

138 WHALLEY AVE. 562-7220

PROUDLY WELCOMES BACK

POLYDOR RECORING ARTISTS

MICHAEL BOLOTIN

FRI 26th
SAT. 27th
DOORS OPEN 8:00

ARRIVE EARLY

AND **BLACKJACK**

ONLY CT. APPEARANCE

IN CONCERT WITH

RAT CITY RECORDING ARTISTS

GOOD RATS

TICKETS AVAILABLE AT DOOR ONLY

A 1980 flyer

(Ahouby/Star File)

1

Dream While You Can

Michael's home town lies roughly seventy miles northeast of Manhattan at a confluence of three small rivers. New Haven, Connecticut, was founded in 1638 by a group of wealthy Puritans led by a minister and a merchant. They raised their city on the site of a former Indian village, Quinnipiac. Circled east and west by hills and bordered on the south by Long Island Sound, New Haven was a bustling port during the 1700s doing brisk business trafficking products manufactured by the state's industrious residents. Except on Sundays. New Haven was the first American city to enact Blue Laws prohibiting Sabbath trade. The city's been on an economic downswing for many years and these days is primarily known for being home to Yale University.

Connecticut has three nicknames. It's called the Constitution State because its colonial laws influenced our Federal government. George Washington christened it the Provision State to honor farmers' herculean efforts providing for his troops throughout the Revolution. Most call it the Nutmeg State, a nickname acquired because Yankee peddlers were reputed to be so slick they could sell wooden nutmegs as real ones to unsuspecting buyers.

With its long history of hard work and strong beliefs, this Connecticut city makes a fitting home for the singer born Michael Bolotin (the family is Russian) on February 26, in the early 1950s.

The exact year is unclear, and Bolton prefers it blurry: "I'm somewhere between 25 and 50. What I like about people not knowing my age is that I get fan mail where people guess so low I feel like putting cash into an envelope."

Bolton probably hit forty in 1993. He's the baby of his family, and a 1992 *People* story gave his brother Orrin and sister Sandra's ages as 43 and 41 respectively. Michael's father, George Bolotin, was an avid Yankee fan and a ward chairman in the Democratic party until his death in 1981. His mom, Helen, came from a theatrical family. Today she works in an adolescent counseling center. Sandra is a social worker. Orrin, who's also a musician, pursues independent projects. By all accounts, the Bolotins were a fairly average middle-class family until his parents divorced when Michael was ten.

1976

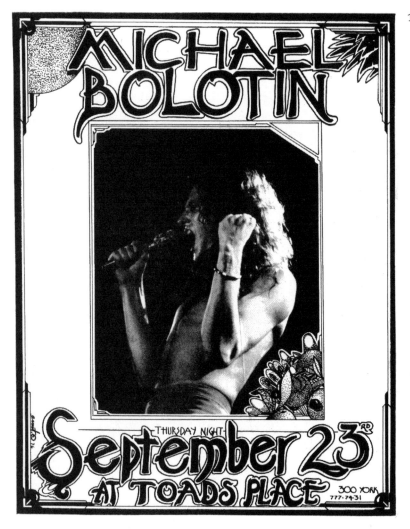

"It was pretty tumultuous," Bolton recalls. "They divorced at a time when there was a real stigma. We were extraordinarily self-conscious about what our parents were going through." Michael lived with Helen, an amateur singer who encouraged his musical aspirations. She taught Michael an esoteric repertoire of songs that he warbled around the house and even in school, mystifying his classmates. Michael's more earthbound dad urged him to pursue a legal career.

For those who follow astrology, it's fascinating that Bolton was born under the most complex sign of the zodiac, Pisces. The twelfth sign represents death and eternity, since it's the composite of all that's gone before. Karmically, Pisceans have cycled through each sign at least once, absorbing their spiritual lessons and traits.

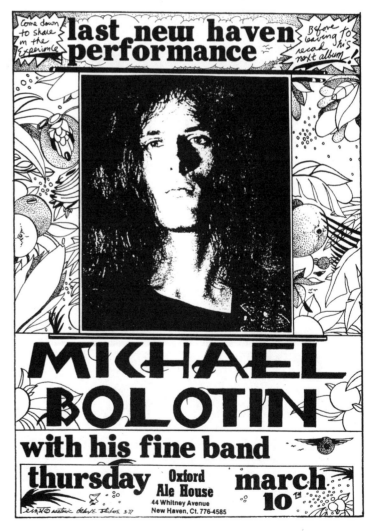

(Chuck Pulin/Star File)

This ad appeared in a local newspaper in 1980.

Many Pisceans are fair-haired and graceful. Their eyes are "full of strange lights," according to astrologer Linda Goodman. They're often plagued with fragile health and surprisingly—at least where Michael's concerned—many suffer from weak lungs! They have boundless imagination which often makes it tough coping with life's mundane realities. They feel things quite deeply.

Michael is true to his Piscean profile in other ways, too: Many Pisceans become performers or religious seekers. They hate confinement of any sort, whether it's actual physical entrapment or invisible mental constraints. Consequently, they'll rarely condemn others' beliefs; theirs is an open-minded, forgiving nature. Pisces' private domain is intensely creative, some say visionary. They're secretive, but charming to a fault as long as you don't divert them from a cherished personal dream. Famous Pisceans include Elizabeth Taylor, Zero Mostel, Chopin, Elizabeth Browning, Rudolph Nureyev, Michelangelo and Albert Einstein.

Michael's mother, Helen, a vivacious, attractive blond, confirms that even as a child Bolton hid his emotions as if they were state secrets and followed his own eccentric course. She was roundly criticized in New Haven for her progressive parenting style. "I lost a lot of friends because of the way I raised him. I

17

believed in live and let live. Bring them up freely and let them do what they want. If they make a mistake, they rectify it and learn from it. I was always going to school to argue with the principal over the length of Michael's hair. I didn't think it was anyone else's business. A lot of my friends thought Michael was a bad example." Instinctively she hit upon the best method for rearing this unique soul, and the continuing closeness of their relationship testifies to the wisdom of her choice.

Michael and his brother Orrin went hand in glove. They even look very much alike. Like a lot of younger kids, Michael modeled himself on the older boy, and together they were a formidable team. "My father not being in the home created a situation where my mother had to try to control two sons who were very strong-willed and had their own agenda." By his own admission, Bolton was a hellraiser. He laughs, "My mother wrote songs. One that should have been a smash was 'You Kids Are Killing Me.' Another was 'I'm Gonna Throw You Outta the House,' and 'You Oughta Have Kids Like You When You Grow Up.' "

Michael was an irreverent kid who turned everything into a joke. On the one hand he was captain of his baseball team. On the other, he was booted out of Sunday school. "I couldn't sit in a class with other people without joking or making other kids laugh and get in trouble with me. Almost everything is funny to me." Bolton's sense of humor is sly. He doesn't telegraph his punch lines with a goofy grin or nudge in the ribs, but lets them slide out, seemingly offhand. He'll wait patiently until you realize it's hilarious, then reward you with a dazzling smile.

Chances are the Bolotin boys inherited their strong wills from dad. "Someone said about Michael's father, 'If he said hello it sounded like an argument,' " said Helen. George was a college football player who pushed his son to excel at sports and cherished dreams that Michael would follow him into business or politics. Instead, Bolton mixed Helen's artistic bent with George's tremendous drive and doggedly pursued his musical career from an early age. As if he had any choice! Bolton claims his urge to write and perform music is innate, uncontrollable—it's been his prime motivation from day one.

When he was seven, Michael's parents rented him a saxophone. He spent hours in front of the mirror pretending to play while actually exercising his vocal cords. Michael intuitively knew voice was his primary instrument. He was enthralled by Orrin's extensive collection of R&B albums and worshipped such singers as Otis Redding, Ray Charles, and Marvin Gaye. Today their work remains his gold standard because, "They sing with feeling. They're not inhibited about expressing emotion."

Michael's never had formal musical training and says, "I still can't read music technically." Later in life he'd take voice lessons to learn to boost his range and power and increase his stamina during long tours. To this day he's very protective of his gift and says, "You become a life support system for this voice."

With Orrin on drums and Michael singing and strumming guitar, the boys began collaborating when Michael was around eleven or twelve. They were "showing up and crashing parties whether they wanted us or not," he recalls. "By the time I was

At a benefit at The Ritz, New York City

(Chuck Pulin/Star File)

(Chuck Pulin/Star File)

(Larry Busacca/Retna)

fifteen I was in the studio making demos." Though under legal drinking age, Michael became a fixture on the New Haven bar circuit—singing the blues. "I was out past my bedtime," he admits.

Thanks to old acquaintances like Ernst Weber, Jr., we can catch a glimpse of Michael's early, struggling years. In the mid-seventies Bolton, his wife, and assorted friends inhabited a colonial-style mansion in New Haven's tony Westville neighborhood. To finance their musical ventures the collective organized a business producing tee shirts decorated with pictures of unicorns, rainbows, seagulls, and clouds. Ernst, a Renaissance man who's currently a freelance artist, video producer, poet, and mechanic, answered an ad for an airbrusher.

He remembers: "I was intrigued because I'd always wanted to learn how to airbrush. You walked up to this huge house with a circular driveway and it was something out of a movie to see all these hippie kind of communal people living inside the walls of a house you'd expect to see a Rolls Royce parked in front of. There was all kinds of music and rehearsals going on here, too. That's how I initially met Michael. From then, one thing led to another with his gigs. He'd say, 'I need a poster. Can you whip something up? I need it yesterday.' Nothing ever changes."

Ernst faced impossible deadlines working on the tee shirts and flyers for Michael's gigs. Often all he had time to do was change the time, venue, and date on a poster before printing and distributing it around town. The tee shirts were an ongoing project as well. Once painted, they were taken to Bolton's manager's mom's house and popped into the oven to "set" the images. More than a few went up in smoke.

Michael has explained that his career was launched by a friend who managed a local band: "He heard me sing 'I Was Born in Chicago.' I sang like an old blues singer, like a forty-five- to fifty-year-old blues singer. My voice was almost the same when I was twelve as it is now. People would always say, 'I can't believe that voice is coming out of you.'"

That early supporter was Richard "Ribs" Friedlander, who convinced Bolton to concentrate on singing rather than playing instruments. "Ribs is really responsible for getting me in the business professionally," said Michael. "He got me into singing songs at high schools and colleges. I was the lead singer of the group called George's Boys," a well-known New Haven group during the sixties.

A short time later, demonstrating incredible determination

and self-possession, Michael dropped out of school to pursue his musical career. He was fourteen years old. "I decided not to fool around and see everything fade away. Looking back, you see that if you took the wrong turn, the dream would have been over. Take the right one or just go straight ahead and everything opens up for you." Even at fourteen, Michael's image and ideas were decidedly unorthodox. Music played in his head, and it seemed logical to pursue it rather than stay in school. It's impossible to imagine that Helen and George were thrilled by this decision, yet Michael appears to have been unstoppable. "I remember, no matter what anybody told me, I had to learn my own way," he says.

Whatever their doubts, Bolton's parents proved staunch allies. Helen Bolotin told *The New York Times* that once George realized Michael was serious about music, "he became his number one fan." This is confirmed by Ernst: "I've read that he wasn't that close to his father when things first got rolling, but I know that in the 1970s [George] would show up at every gig. He'd walk in with his cane and look around and they'd exchange glances and chat. If things weren't great between them before, things certainly came around. It was nice to see that."

Michael also calls George "my biggest fan." He says George saw success in his future long before Michael believed in it himself. "He'd look at me and say, 'You're gonna be big, big, big.' Never one big!"

Helen adds, "We always knew Michael would succeed. It was a question of when, not if, even in the days he couldn't feed his family and was getting eviction notices. He was always so focused on what he wanted. He was very secretive, very private, very shy." No one observing this determined teenager guessed it would take so long to hit paydirt.

(Gary Gershoff/Retna)

2

Welcome to the World

Impetuous as it was to quit school, Michael Bolton had every reason to believe, at age fifteen, that his career was well-launched. Midway through 1968 he traveled to Berkeley, California with Joy—another band renowned for their cult following in New Haven, especially among Yalies. Joy landed a contract to record a single for Epic, a division of Columbia Records. Since he was underage, Michael's mom co-signed the contract. The single was a Bolton original, "Bah Bah Song." It made minor ripples in Connecticut, where the band was known, but bombed everywhere else.

By the time he recalled this disaster for his 1992 TV special, Michael could afford to be philosophical, though his youthful excitement and subsequent disappointment came through. "I'd never really been in a recording studio before. Didn't know what I was doing, but I got a call back from Epic records, they wanted to see us live. They came and signed me to a singles deal. I remember feeling like 'I made it—look at this, it's amazing, I made it.' In one year it was over and gone, but I had been bitten, I had a taste of what I really wanted to do."

Bolton says he found the equivalent of a Dear John letter in his mailbox one day. Columbia wrote: "You are now free to sign with whoever you like." He was only sixteen and he was washed up.

Education takes many forms. Bolton's Epic adventure taught him a home truth that retained its value throughout his career. "I realized the record company's primary concern was the song and the voice, not the backing musicians. I was the writer and the singer, so I knew there'd be interest in me if I could deliver."

Bolton started composing original music even before he turned professional. He told *Seventeen* his first big, inspiring crush occurred when he was thirteen, smitten with an older woman of nineteen. "She thought I was cute, so we used to hang out together. I was her little sidekick." Their friendship prompted a love song, and Michael's journey as a chronicler of the heart's vagaries had begun.

In 1970 Bolton ventured back to California, this time heading south to Los Angeles, where Richard Friedlander ran a vegetarian restaurant. By now Michael was a vegetarian himself. He told Ernst, "I never realized that when you eat meat somebody had to chop the heads off of cows, stop their life just so you can enjoy the taste and texture of meat. Meat is no good for you. It kills constantly. The meat on the market is fake, full of chemicals. At the time of death an animal experiences pain and fear and their adrenalin is flowing intensely—all this goes into you, too."

Friedlander's restaurant attracted an arty, musical crowd, including George Harrison and members of the Beach Boys. "Ribs" often bragged about his young friend's astonishing vocal strength, and these well-connected patrons encouraged Friedlander to make demo tapes in order to court producers. Initially Bolton worked with the short-lived Pentagram Records, which went belly up during his recording sessions.

He was more successful auditioning for Joe Cy at Shelter Records in 1971. Like Joshua blowing down the walls of Jericho, Michael's powerhouse delivery penetrated through sheetrock and insulation to grab the attention of Denny Cordell in the adjoining office. Cordell invited Bolton to join Leon Russell's tour as an opening act. When Bolton agreed, Cordell said, "Pack tonight. You leave first thing in the morning!"

Bolton was awestruck by Leon Russell's talented musical crew and dreamed of working with them himself. "Six months later I got flown out to Shelter's studios in Tulsa, and Leon's band backed me up on some tapes I did. I also recorded with musicians that were with Eric Clapton. I took those tapes to New York and got a deal with RCA Records." It's a testament to Shelter's generosity and belief in the youngster's talent that they gave so much of themselves for demos he'd shop around to other labels.

(Ernst Weber, Jr.)

Michael, circa 1970

The man responsible for signing Bolton to RCA was Stephen Holden, now an influential cabaret reviewer at *The New York Times*. From 1974–76, Holden was a low-level A&R man at RCA. In a 1987 *Times* article, Holden recalled "discovering" twenty-two-year-old Bolton—still Bolotin—in 1974. On the basis of a strong demo, Holden invited Michael and his two managers—one was brother Orrin—for an interview. Holden thought the trio looked like a bunch of penniless hippies. Both managers were in thrall to Bolton's talent and came away with tremendous, contagious faith in his star power. Amusingly enough, they suggested billing him with just one name—Michael. Holden vetoed that affectation.

Holden was mesmerized by Bolton's demo: "[It] gave me chills from the moment I put it on." He firmly believed Michael

had the requisite good looks, good material, and presence to make the grade. Michael's vocals sounded "like a junior Joe Cocker. But along with a rock blues ferocity, his singing had a heart-tugging sweetness. I was enraptured by his version of an original ballad, 'Dream While You Can,' that during the hundreds of times I listened to it always seemed to float mystically out of the huge speakers in my office."

Holden signed Michael to a two-record deal that paid a $10,000 advance. The first album's budget was a low $40,000. Union restrictions made it necessary to record at RCA's New York studios, and work began in December of 1974.

Holden contends this budget was too small to allow Bolton's best effort and regrets that the company didn't get behind his discovery for reasons both political and financial. If Bolton were signed by an upper level honcho instead of a peon, Holden speculated, he would have been backed by heavy promtion including advertising and a full-scale PR blitz that might have altered history. (Holden also tried signing punk poetess Patti Smith, but RCA didn't bite, so she wound up under contract at Clive Davis's Arista label.)

Musicians on the eponymous first album, *Michael Bolotin*, included Jim Horn and David Sanborn on saxophone, Wayne Perkins on guitar, Bernard "Pretty" Purdie on drums (who played for James Brown, Aretha Franklin, and Dizzy Gillespie), Wilbur Bascomb playing bass, percussionist Andy Newmark, and Patrick "Reverend" Henderson on keyboards. Mary McCreary (on the verge of marrying Leon Russell) and Marcy Levy sang background vocals. The record was produced by Joe Cy.

These were heavy-duty talents for a young unknown singer to hook up with. David Sanborn's career was just breaking, and today he's gone on to become a popular star. During the Bolton sessions guitarist Wayne Perkins auditioned with the Rolling Stones for Mick Taylor's slot. He played on their "Black and Blue" album but ultimately lost the job to Ron Wood.

Michael penned eight originals for this eleven-song release and covered "Time Is on My Side," by N. Meade, the tune the Rolling Stones immortalized. But Bolton's rendition has a flavor all its own. He starts with a big, blasting shout and sings hard throughout, evincing the same outgoing style he's criticized for (and adored for) today.

Bolton's second RCA album, *Every Day of My Life*, was produced by savvy Jack Richardson, who masterminded hits for Canadian superstars the Guess Who and produced Poco and Alice

Cooper. They recorded at the Nimbus 9 studios in Toronto using local musical talent. Bolton only contributed four originals this time. He covered tunes like "Rocky Mountain Way," by Joe Walsh, Burton Cummings's "These Eyes," and that perennial favorite, "Dancing in the Street." He regretted not fighting to put more of his own songs on the album. Covering the old Martha Reeves hit was "mainly commercialism," he admitted to Ernst. "It's not really expressing what I want to express."

Supporting musicians were Henderson on piano, Jan Mullaney on organ, Billy Elworthy on guitars, Gary Ferraro on bass, drummer Jay Michaels, and special guest Papa John Creach on fiddle. Colina Phillips, Charon Lee Williams, and Rhonda Silver sang background harmonies.

The second album cover is a painting done from a photograph. It promotes the artist as "sensitive poet-songwriter." Michael is somber. His already trademark locks flow in an imaginary breeze as he hunches over his guitar. The look is very James Taylor, very soulful. Fans eager to hear these early Bolton efforts (and see this image) should look for the 1991 BMG reissue, *Michael Bolotin: The Early Years*, a twelve-cut CD featuring the best of both RCA albums.

How do these old tracks sound? Drummer Andy Newmark quipped, "The kid sings his little ass off." The mood is very seventies, reflecting the heavy influence of Russell's southern-style rock, Joe Cocker's *Mad Dogs and Englishmen* sound, plus hints of Derek and the Dominos, Gregg Allman, and other bluesy Southern strains so popular during that era.

The songs themselves are a mixed bag. Like his current work, they rely less on intricate, image-laden lyrics but stand or fall on the strength of a few simple thoughts, powerfully delivered. Then as now, many of Bolton's strongest compositions are ballads. Stephen Holden's favorite cut, "Dream While You Can," lives up to the raves. It's a haunting lullaby exhorting a little child to dream, fly, and be free before childhood slips away. The song takes on deeper meaning when you realize it's written and performed by someone not far from childhood himself. Bolton's husky baritone sounds truly wistful. Was he already feeling walls close in on him? Perhaps it was the pressure of his early marriage and fatherhood. Maybe Michael felt weary. Here he was still unproven at twenty-two, in spite of the excitement he generated as a teen.

Close your eyes during this surprisingly sophisticated ballad and you can't tell the age or race of the singer, making it easy to believe Bolton's claim that bar audiences "would do double takes.

Here was a skinny little kid with hair down to his waist sounding like a fifty-year-old black blues singer. And I was just singing what I loved to sing."

Bolton's version of "These Eyes"—a huge success for the Guess Who—magnificently showcases his strong voice. Singing a slowed-down version, Michael manages to convey anger, sadness, and torment simultaneously. Background violins enhance the mournful quality of his rendition.

Another strong original ballad is "If I Had Your Love." Again Bolton shows a fondness for flight imagery, but now he's crooning to a woman. He begins in a near whisper, listing "ifs," building to a wrenching plea, "If I only had your love/There'd be no if I hads at all." It's an early glimpse of a now-standard Bolton theme—love's redemptive power to heal, make whole, restore order amid chaos.

On the subject of recurring themes, Bolton's funky, up-tempo song "Tell Me How You Feel" asks his woman how their love can be real if she won't express what's on her mind and in her heart. It's a precursor of his late 80s question, "How can we be lovers if we can't be friends?"

"You Mean More to Me" is an if-you-need-me-holler tune that adds little to the genre. Michael promises his woman that their love is bigger and better than anything previously imaginable. "Give Me a Reason" is a perky number exploring the irrational nature of love. It finds Bolton asking a faithless woman why he keeps loving her despite lies and abuse. "It's Just a Feeling" covers similar ground—I don't know what love *is*, exactly, but I'm up to my neck in it, he sings. "Your Love" tells of an affair that's "turning me around/I'm lost, don't want to be found," played out against a funky boogie-woogie piano and sax riff that reinforces Bolton's message: love may be confusing but it's *fun* confusion.

At the time Michael wasn't one hundred percent satisfied with the RCA albums. Still that dissatisfaction was something of a comfort; it gave him new goals to strive for. Like many young artists Michael feared satisfaction equalled complacency. He felt it would take persistence and rigorous high standards to achieve the former without succumbing to the latter. "I do think that eventually I will be satisfied," he concluded, "but contrary to what most people say, I don't think that once I [do] that it will stop me from getting any better."

Michael was terrified that a record label would enslave him to the fatuous pop tunes that characterized seventies Top 40 radio. "There's a lot of music that isn't doing anything, it's just mak-

30

Michael outside Radio City Music Hall in New York City before the Grammy Rehearsals with Pierre Cossett, producer of the Grammys

(Chuck Pulin/Star File)

ing people go up and down . . . it's not taking people any place of any value to me. . . ." For Bolton, music that's worthwhile must inspire an emotional journey.

Throughout the early 1970s Michael Bolton performed at roadhouses, proms, private parties, and other small venues. "I was in bar bands and we were doing Chicago Blues, Junior Wells, and Paul Butterfield," he says. Ernst recalls that gigs came in spurts, depending upon Michael's finances. It's expensive to assemble a band and sound equipment, not to mention transportation to clubs. Plus, Michael worried he'd overstay his welcome around town, so he consciously limited exposure in area clubs.

"Michael played two good New Haven clubs a lot—Toad's Place and the Arcadia Ballroom, which was the predecessor to the Great American Music Hall, owned by Bobby Lucabello, who also owned the Oxford Ale House, a smaller club," says Ernst. With an eye toward posterity, Michael asked Ernst to photograph the gigs. Typically, Michael paid for the film and developing, leaving Ernst to choose his shots, many of which are published here for the first time.

Not only photography, but *everything* was done for pennies in those days. "Everybody was on the low economic end, searching for their muse and doing what they felt was right even if it didn't earn money," Ernst remembers. Even so, members of the Westville household maintained a loose open door policy. Guests were assured of a welcome. There was always plenty of fruit, vegetarian snacks, and organic munchies on hand. The group continued churning out airbrushed tee shirts, and Michael bolstered his income by giving singing lessons near Chapel Street, downtown. In between he found time to rehearse at a vast second-floor space in the former Hamilton Clock Factory just outside city center.

These days Bolton has assembled a collection of expensive sports cars, but back then he drove a succession of old, decaying heaps, frequently calling upon Ernst to patch them up so they'd run a few miles more. Ernst says Michael either didn't know much about cars or simply didn't pay a whole lot of attention to

In concert at the
Jones Beach Arena,
New York City

(Chuck Pulin/Star File)

their care and upkeep. Sometimes all they needed was an oil change to stop sputtering and start purring.

Once or twice, however, the band traveled to a gig by limo. Ernst laughs about this now. "I think Michael's manager knew somebody who had a limo or an old Caddy and said wouldn't it be fun. . . . We'd fit *everybody* into the car! It wasn't a grandiose gesture, but it was funny. Like, 'Here comes the limo!' but it's not a new stretch limo, just a funky caddy with a padded vinyl top. It wasn't even the right color!"

Bolton's strong local following trailed him on the bar circuit. "There was always an enthusiastic crowd, and his set was energetic to the max. He played originals and covers. At the time, originals were hard for people to swallow because most club-goers have a jukebox kind of mentality. They want to hear their favorite songs. Michael was very fortunate in that his songwriting abilities were just so intense that his original stuff was accepted immediately with respect and admiration. But when he played somebody else's song, he owned that song. Like he'd always start the gig with 'Rocky Mountain Way,' by Joe Walsh. When Michael played it, it was 'Bye, Joe. Thanks.' Michael's version was a killer. He was definitely a phenomenal musician."

Reviewers for small publications are the best source for news on little-known club acts. Those who caught Bolton were impressed by his ability to move a crowd. The *Berkeley Press/Star News* said: "It's just impossible to convey the excitement on record. Unless you've seen him, you can't imagine the intensity that captures a live audience." *The Aquarian* raved, "They screamed, they shouted, they danced and stood on their chairs in order to get a better look at who and what was happening on stage." *Match Entertainment Guide* enthused, "A super star, Michael Bolotin *is* music."

Michael played a mean lead guitar at these seventies gigs. "In those days Michael was accessible," says Ernst. "He was a hard-working musician and an excellent guitarist, which is one of the things I miss now. I keep hoping at one of these concerts he's going to break out his guitar and do a rock and roll song. Would the crowd go nuts or boo or what? Back then he did the ballads, but he was a hard rocker who played a lot of gritty rhythm and blues."

Then as now, Bolton loved wearing suits on stage. He'd yet to hone the emotive—some say histrionic—style he's famous for, but it wasn't unusual for Bolton to "finish big" by leaping high, then crashing dramatically to his knees.

Inevitably there's some bad blood between managers and musicians still working in New Haven and Michael Bolton—at least on the New Haven side. Many feel he's abandoned his roots, turned his back on old friends who helped him get started. Several musicians who worked with Michael in the seventies wouldn't be interviewed for this book. Remarkably, they defy obvious expectations; because they have nothing good to say, they'd rather keep quiet. That's either the sign of a true gentleman or fear of provoking Bolton's wrath. Rumor has it one former compadre has oft-pierced Michael Bolton dartboards adorning his office.

To Michael's bitter disappointment both RCA albums were commercial failures. He felt their artistic merit was underappreciated. In 1976 he insisted the first album should have been a hit: "I think it's better than a lot of stuff I hear on the radio. It has better energy and some really good songs." *Rolling Stone* agreed: "His soulful songwriting and strong backup provide a striking debut." *Riverside Press* raved, "His album ranks as the year's top debut, and as one of the year's very finest albums by anybody." By 1988 Bolton recanted, telling Robert K. Oermann, "Save your money. [Those albums] were me learning about my voice."

Although he feared betraying himself with commercial pop music, Bolton wound up singing jingles for Leber & Kreb to keep his family afloat. Mike Spoerndle, the owner of New Haven's premier club, Toad's Place, remembers Bolton sang a Budweiser commercial, his basso voice booming "B-B-B-B-Bud!" Even then some of the New York advertising crowd bugged Michael to chop his hair. He'd return from New York recording sessions confused, asking the folks back home, "What do you think?" Most echoed Ernst, who counseled, "Keep it if you like it."

Around the same time he signed with RCA, Bolton married twenty-three-year-old Maureen McGuire. Now divorced, he's legally forbidden to discuss their marriage, but he wasn't exaggerating when he told *People*, "I was very young." The pair were teens when they met in 1970. Maureen worked in a New Haven record store where Michael shopped. They dated for five years, then wed. By 1976 they had their first daughter, Isa, followed in short order by two more girls, Holly and Taryn.

During the early 1970s Michael, Maureen, and their circle of friends were members of the Divine Light Mission, a worldwide Hindu-based cult dedicated to promoting the Guru Maharaj Ji's "knowledge." Michael was searching for spiritual enlightenment. Linda Goodman explains it's typical of Pisces to explore art or

34

At the Paramount
Theater in New York
City

(Chuck Pulin/Star File)

drugs or meditation and religious retreat as an antidote to life's
harsher elements. Liz Greene, a London-based psychologist/as-
trologer, adds that Pisces is the sign of mystics, those longing for
transcendent experiences.

DLM stressed the sacred relationship between the guru—a
boy of 15—and his disciples. Its popularity quickly spread, at-

tracting more than 50,000 members, mostly white, middle-class kids under thirty. Many DLM followers had "done" the counter-culture and the sixties drug scene but were still searching for the missing element that would bring spiritual peace.

Followers of DLM were called "premies" and taught to employ four techniques of meditation in order to absorb the guru's knowledge—wisdom he claimed to have received, like Moses, directly from God. According to the guru, successful meditation bestowed celestial light and music, internal vibrations, and the taste of mystic nectar. He claimed to be God's terrestrial representative whose ambitious mission was nothing less than establishing world peace.

Highly sophisticated, DLM was incorporated as a non-profit, non-sectarian, tax-exempt organization. From branches throughout the country linked by then state-of-the-art telexes, DLM published two magazines, *And It Is Divine* and *Divine Times*, made promotional films, and produced a pamphlet, *Who is Guru Maharaj Ji?* a summary of his teachings combined with glowing testimonials from followers.

Since it was primarily member-funded, the DLM had to feed like a shark, constantly hunting for new disciples who were then encouraged to donate 30 percent of their earnings to the mission. The sale of recycled goods provided additional income.

Like many charismatic cult leaders, the Guru lived amidst contradictions. He preached that ego was evil and dangerous, the source of negativity, strife, and bellicosity. Yet this teenager and self-proclaimed "Perfect Master" lived the high life, surrounding himself with flashy electronic equipment, expensive real estate, and a chauffeured Rolls Royce.

Michael and Maureen were premies. Ernst asked whether Michael's refusal to eat meat was an outgrowth of his spiritual practices, which included meditation, Michael replied, "In one way . . . I became sensitive to the fact that there are other things in life besides my own desires. . . . The most important thing I've found going on inside me is my life—the fact that I'm alive, the source of my life, the energy inside me that makes me go on living, keeps my heart beating and my lungs breathing."

He drew a parallel between this life force and his compulsion to create. "Music itself is just something I can't do without. . . . It's constantly calling for my attention. When a song starts being written through me, it's like childbirth."

(Michael Putland/Retna)

3

Can't Hold On, Can't Let Down

Punk engulfed Great Britain in the mid-seventies but took longer to cross the Atlantic. By the time most Americans knew of the Sex Pistols, the Clash, and other nihilist rock groups, the decade was winding down. American rebels hopped the bandwagon with glee, but punk was never a unifying force on this side of the Great Pond. Though punk poetry readings and art happenings coexisted with more traditional entertainment on the New Haven club scene, Michael Bolton never embraced anarchy or razored his hair. Instead, to the surprise of many, he turned up at the helm of a hard rock ensemble named Blackjack.

Blackjack, a solid quartet of seasoned professionals, consisted of Sandy Gennaro on drums, Bruce Kulick on guitars, Jimmy Haslip on bass, and Michael's vocals. The group came together in autumn of 1978. They were a straight-from-central-casting seventies rock ensemble down to their tight shirts, tight jeans, and requisite stripes of black eyeliner. Bolton's "career consultant" at this time was Phil Lorito, operating under the aegis of MBO Artists, Inc./Artists One located in Farmingville, New York. Bookings for the band were handled by I.C.M.'s New York office.

Blackjack released two widely ignored albums for Polydor. The first debuted on June 18, 1979. Named after the band, *Blackjack* featured: "Love Me Tonight," "Fallin'," "Without Your Love,"

"I'm Aware of Your Love," "For You," "Heart of Stone," "The Night Has Me Calling," "Countin' on You," and "Heart of Mine." The producer was Tom Dowd. Rehearsal and recording sessions took place from October through May at Full Tilt Sound Studios in Manhattan; Long View Farm in North Brookfield, Massachusetts; and in Miami, Florida.

The second album, entitled *Worlds Apart*, was produced by Eddy Offard at his Woodstock, New York, studio. Songs included "My World Is Empty Without You," "Love Is Hard to Find," "Stay," "Airwaves," "Maybe It's the Power of Love," "Welcome to the World," "Breakaway," "Really Wanna Know," "Sooner or Later,"

(Ernst Weber, Jr.)

and "She Wants You Back." The cover of this 1980 release depicts a desolate rock-strewn landscape overshadowed by heavy clouds sliced by a jagged bolt of lightning. Ernst Weber, Jr. still has his autographed copy, which Bolton inscribed: "Ernst, Love and happiness for you through the madness. Always, Michael."

A decade later, in 1990, PolyGram cashed in on Bolton's rising popularity by assembling a twenty-cut "best of Blackjack" CD. Sony got wind of this and sent a stern note prohibiting PolyGram from trading on the name Michael Bolton—adopted in 1982 after signing with CBS—for publicity purposes. Aside from monetary issues, the fear was that innocent record buyers eager for Bolton product would be suckered into believing these Blackjack tracks were new.

PolyGram packaged their CD cleverly. The cover features all four musicians clearly identified. Bolton is Bolotin, of course, but his photo is slightly set off from the rest. Unlike the other band members sporting tight, striped polo shirts, Michael is wearing a flowing white poet's shirt. Was it a sartorial nod toward his songwriter status?

Blackjack's music isn't true heavy metal. It lacks the relentless noisy drive of Led Zeppelin, Metallica, Def Leppard, or AC/DC. It's not obsessed with classic metal themes of death and destruction, devil worship, sex, or drugs. Actually most of the uptempo tracks sound like Michael Bolton singing Foreigner tunes. "Feels Like the First Time" has a lot in common with Blackjack's "Love Is Hard to Find." Some likened Blackjack to Bruce Springsteen, but the lyrics lack Bruce's density and intelligence. The music itself is far too slick to warrant comparison to Springsteen's first trio of albums. Comparison to Bad Company feels more apt.

As always, Bolton sings about love found and lost. But gone is the Southern bluesman, replaced by a generic white rocker. For instance, the ballad "Stay" showcases Bolton's raw, aching vocals, but now they're pit against tsunami-force drums instead of acoustic guitar. To his credit, Michael holds his own. Big, crashing drums and fast, loud guitar solos are hallmarks of both albums.

One has to wonder why Blackjack didn't become a megagroup like Foreigner, which achieved enormous popularity and wealth thanks to nonstop hits and successful tours—the resemblance is so strong. Was it poor publicity or lackluster distribution on Polydor's behalf? Internal strife? Did Bolton's longing for the spotlight make him restive hidden in a band? His first two solo efforts for Columbia sound similar enough to Blackjack to invite the question. At any event, by fall of 1980 lawyers for Haslip, Ku-

(Gary Gershoff/Retna)

(Gary Gershoff/Retna)

lick, and Gennaro were petitioning Polydor and MBO Enterprises for their clients' release from all contractual obligations.

Michael Bolton hit bottom. After years of nonstop touring, recording, and songwriting, he was destitute. He couldn't pay rent on his two-bedroom walkup. The young family subsisted on macaroni and cheese and frozen broccoli. In those days they didn't ask *what* they could buy the girls but *which one* they could afford to clothe.

He told *People*, "It's not hard for me to access this view of that apartment. I'm sitting at the kitchen table wondering how I'm going to pay my rent and feed my children. . . . I would go in and out of the most depressing thoughts, trying to imagine some way out of the situation. That was the darkest period, when I didn't see any light at the end of the tunnel.

"Rent checks were bouncing and I was getting official eviction notices. I remember . . . just staring out the window and wondering if I could get another deal."

When you don't have a steady job and paycheck, the slightest alteration in plans can spell economic disaster. If a gig was cancelled by bad weather or a single bombed, Bolton wound up broke again. He counts himself lucky to have retained a strong local following. With a phone call he was often able to arrange last-minute acoustic gigs to put a few dollars in his pocket.

Several management groups had pieces of Bolton. One, New Haven's Savoy Agency, helped Michael advertise for opening acts to support some of his more organized local appearances. Dennis Nardella, a vocalist and harmonica player, answered the ad on behalf of Rival, a pop group still active in Connecticut. Though the band plays regularly, Rival has never been its members' sole source of income. Nardella manages a condominium complex, owns and operates a recording studio, and creates a cable access show.

"You could pretty much speak to Michael back then," Dennis says. "I talked to him, sent him some tapes, and he gave us our first job. He was playing a lot of jobs in Connecticut trying to make a living. Everyone in our band had other jobs, but music was how he survived."

Dennis remembers that in the early 80s they earned about twenty-five dollars for a gig—for the entire band! Nardella insists Bolton's cut wasn't much better. "He was trying to support himself and his family and keep expenses down. We played about a dozen shows all over the state. Rival did original rock, a mixture of progressive stuff and pop. I think Bolton liked us because we

always showed up on time and we weren't temperamental. I admit we did learn one of his songs as a riff and started doing it for sound checks in front of the crew. It was kind of a goof."

Dennis's one complaint was that Michael never saw Rival play because he didn't turn up until the last minute. Rival might take the stage around ten to warm up the crowd. Bolton arrived closer to 11:30, nearer his turn to perform. Nardella says Bolton already acted the star despite his dire straits. "He was always nice, but he was always a star. Michael didn't set up equipment or do sound checks." After considerable begging, Bolton finally caught Rival's act and hung out with the band backstage one night.

In Dennis's view Michael wasn't the accomplished showman he is today. "Michael would just glare at the audience," he recalls. Unlike Ernst, he rates Bolton only average on the guitar and says, "His voice, if you weren't used to it, was really strange." Members

(Gary Gershoff/Retna)

of Rival didn't quite fathom Michael's work, though they sensed he was on the move and, rumor had it, on the verge of a new record deal. Dennis says, "He had name recognition, but it wasn't as if people were lining up and screaming for him. They knew they'd see good music; he had a good band."

Though nearly ten years had passed, Bolton still launched his act with "Rocky Mountain Way," a song whose bold opening chords make great entrance music. His set included originals and cover versions of tunes by Joe Cocker, Bob Seeger, even Wings.

As Dennis remembers it, Maureen Bolotin was responsible for Michael's first frizzy perm. "One of the guys in Rival was going to hairdresser school and Bolton's wife was trying to do that, too. This guy said his wife used to experiment on Michael's hair and it's never been the same since." These days Michael won't name names, but says he's been a patron of the same New York salon for many years.

The last gig Rival opened for Bolton occurred at Toad's Place. "Around here that's *the* club," explains Dennis. Indeed, Toad's, located at 300 York Street, has long been a prestigious venue attracting everyone from the Rolling Stones and Billy Joel to local bands on the rise. The crowd's a blend of townies and students from New Haven's three universities: Yale, Albertus Magnus College, and Southern Connecticut State College.

At first Rival wasn't invited to this gig. Unfair, they cried. "We've trooped all over the state playing less prestigious clubs— give us a chance." Dennis remembers: "A lot of people told us we'd never make it to Toad's as Rival. Michael was going to play, so we asked if we could open. He said it wasn't up to him. Finally I got a call one day—you always recognized his voice, deep and husky. He said, 'You wanna play Toad's?' Michael said we'd get a raise, fifty dollars this time. That was our first time playing Toad's and it was really exciting. Then it kind of ended. It was Bolton's last big local tour to support himself. After that he didn't play here on a regular basis once his big albums came out. Now he's headlining at the Coliseum!"

Does Dennis begrudge Michael's success? Definitely not! "I'm a fan. I think the other old-timers are in denial. Michael was nice to play with and it's good to see his success, it gives musicians hope. You *can* make it big if you work hard enough. Bolton's music isn't ground-breaking, but it's infectious. You can't argue with five million albums! This proves where ten years can take somebody."

(Michael Putland/Retna)

4

Back on His Feet Again

Salvation came via Louis Levin, who bought out Michael's management contract in 1982 and negotiated a two-part deal with Columbia (now under the Sony umbrella). Michael's new deal included an all-important songwriting element plus a recording contract. He officially shortened Bolotin to Bolton and set about creating his first CBS album, appropriately named *Michael Bolton*, released in 1983.

The cover shot of *Michael Bolton* is a harbinger of poses to come. He's wearing a leather jacket over bare skin, flashing chest hair. Fluffy curls tumble down to his shoulders. His supernatural carved-in-granite cheekbones fairly burst out in three-D. Michael stares straight into the lens; traces of a smile caught coming or going linger around his mouth.

This nine-cut album produced by Gerry Block with Michael assisting was recorded at Sigma Sound Studios in Manhattan after rehearsals throughout the summer of 1982. The tracks are "Fools Game," "She Did the Same Thing," "Hometown Hero," "Can't Hold On, Can't Let Go," "Fighting for My Life," "Paradise," "Back in My Arms Again," "Carrie," and "I Almost Believed You." With the exception of Holland-Dozier-Holland's "Back in My Arms Again," Michael wrote or co-wrote every track.

Initially Bolton wanted to re-record "Without Your Love" for his Columbia debut. Letters flew between the legal firm of Peter

S. Shukat (on behalf of Leber-Krebs) and PolyGram Records requesting clearance to record the song before the time on its restriction ran out. Executives at PolyGram felt they were in a position to be generous, since the tune had never been successful. Nevertheless, it didn't turn up on *Michael Bolton*.

The album reunites Michael with Blackjack alumni Bruce Kulick, as well as Kulick's brother Bob, both on guitar. Other guitarists were Craig Brooks, Mark Clarke, Bolton, and special guest Aldo Nova. Mark Mangold, Scott Zito, and Doug Katsaros play synthesizers. So does Michael's old crony Jan Mullaney, who doubles on piano and organ. Drums were tackled by Michael Braun and Chuck Burgi.

Bolton dedicated this work to the memory of his dad, who passed away in 1981. Inside he thanked family and friends, along with Mike Sprindel [sic] of Toad's—allegedly the inspiration for "Hometown Hero," a song about becoming an overnight success after years of hard work and the special delight that comes from returning in triumph to your starting point. He also thanked Sally's Pizza, located at 237 Wooster Street. Their pies were so scrumptious and addictive that Michael had them shipped via Federal Express to gigs around the country.

(Ernst Weber, Jr.)

Michael made his first video for "Fools Game," which topped AOR playlists. Even so, this "debut" album is largely forgettable. Every track is identically arranged, delivered, and produced. All the songs begin with a drum/guitar flourish and erupt in a wall-of-sound multi-voice chorus. Heavy reliance on synthesizers further dehumanizes the project. Though the tunes are perky and hum-able, once final chords are struck they fade from your memory banks until the next cut prompts that musical question, "Haven't I heard this already?" It's a collection of perfectly serviceable factory goods instead of individually crafted pieces.

Michael's version of "Back in My Arms Again" takes a sledgehammer to memories of the wispy harmonies of Diana Ross and the Supremes. He pumps this Holland-Dozier-Holland classic full of steroids, adds a guitar solo, and renders it indistinct from everything else in this collection. Only the booming power ballad "I Almost Believed You" hints at Bolton's current output because it slows the tempo and focuses on his exceptionally strong voice.

Bolton's 1985 album, *Everybody's Crazy*, is out of print. On his TV special Michael dismissed *Crazy* as a departure and a failure. "In 1985 I made a record for Columbia that was a hard rock record that a lot of people thought was going to be *the* big record for Michael Bolton, and it wasn't." Anyone holding a copy should stash this collector's item in a bank vault.

The single "Everybody's Crazy" turned up in the movie *Back to School*. Michael also made a video for this song that shows the band performing against giant screens displaying images of real life wackiness, including a man juggling chainsaws. *People* loved it. They called Bolton a second-string rock star with a first-class clip. The album also features Michael's version of "Desperate Heart," later covered by Starship.

Apparently Columbia never worried about their investment in Michael. Someday, somehow, they reasoned, he'll hit his groove. Or as Bolton explained in *USA Today*: "I've always had people around me saying things of support. That second album was the heaviest record I'd ever made. And while we were talking about it at the label, they were already saying, 'If this doesn't work, here's what we think you should do with the next one. The next one.'"

Listening to this early work, it's easy to understand why reviewers joked about Michael's "leather-lunged Mister Macho sound of high-power rock . . . honed to glistening agony." Critics dismissed the early CBS albums as grade B output, yet no one ignored Michael's voice. Nearly all made favorable noises about

(Ernst Weber, Jr.)

(Wasyluk)

(Steve Granitz/Retna)

the promise in this strong multi-octave instrument. Meanwhile, Bolton toured as an opening act for heavy metal performers like Krocus and Ozzy Osbourne. His fans were teenage guys who shot their fists in the air crying "Bolton rules!" during his sets.

The theme of opposition runs throughout Michael's life. Now it surfaced in the schism between his unsuccessful albums and growing recognition as an able songwriter. "Some of my other music started really catching on, the songs I was writing for people like the Pointer Sisters and Kenny Rogers. Laura Branigan had a hit with 'How Am I Supposed to Live Without You?' " Suddenly Bolton tunes were hot properties.

He penned "Can't Keep Runnin' " for Gregg Allman and "Heartbeat," for the Pointer Sisters. "Desperate Heart" was covered by Starship, "We're Not Makin' Love Anymore" by Barbra Streisand. He wrote "Forever" with Paul Stanley of Kiss. Joe Cocker sang "Living Without Your Love" on his 1986 album. Country artists like Gary Morris and T. Graham Brown sang Bolton originals, as did Eric Carmen and Jennifer Rush.

Though he's been writing and performing original material since childhood, Michael claims he was shocked when his compositions hit a motherlode of solid gold. He thought, "Wow, this is easy. You are saying my rent check won't bounce? You're saying I don't have to eat frozen broccoli anymore? I had a talent I didn't even know about."

Surely Michael believed in his abilities. After all, he dropped out of school to pursue a career. Perhaps he worried that the songs couldn't stand alone without his voice to support them. Or was he simply being ingenuous?

Songwriting isn't difficult for Bolton, but like everyone with a talent, he struggles to remain fresh and inspired. He told *Seventeen*: "Lyrics are the toughest to write because you have to say something in a new way that's often already been said. Compelling things worth writing about hit hard and mean a lot. It's nice to hear 'I love you. I honestly love you,' but nothing is as simple as all that."

Things were looking up for Michael Bolton, yet he still had a ways to go. All of a sudden he was a famous *songwriter* but an unknown singer. Though Branigan topped the charts with "How Am I Supposed To Live Without You" in 1983, it was another four years before Bolton would triumph as a performer.

(A. Berliner/Gamma Liaison)

5 Take a Look at My Face

The *Hunger*, a breakthrough album designed to establish Bolton as a crooner, proved a well-calculated turning point. The album yielded his all-important first Top 20 hit as a singer, "That's What Love Is All About," and won Michael a radically different audience—older, female, fanatical.

Stephen Holden ran into Michael on the street in Manhattan just before *The Hunger*'s 1987 release. Fully thirteen years had passed since Holden "discovered" him. Bolton said, "This is going to be the album."

"Ballads!" insisted Holden. "It's got to have ballads. You were always a ballad singer."

"Just wait until you hear," replied Bolton confidently.

What compelled Bolton to re-evaluate the road not taken? Considering the many indications that his fortune lay in ballads, a better question is, What took him so long?

Signs were everywhere and they weren't subtle. For instance, Michael was a feature on the Manhattan club scene, bouncing between Nirvana and the China Club, jamming until dawn with musician friends. Among unfamiliar colleagues it can be tough settling on songs everyone knows—originals may be out of the question. Easier to rely on the ever-popular soul and R&B classics that were Bolton's first love. Otis Redding's "Dock of the Bay" was a staple of this impromptu playlist. Bolton recalls, "The response

(Wasyluk)

(Wasyluk)

(Wasyluk)

was unbelievable the first time we did it, but later people came up and said I should cut it. After enough people suggested it, I took the hint."

There were other hints. "The secretaries at my management firm were always telling me I should put the songs I was giving away on my albums, but I still didn't realize where my power was," admits Michael.

Ultimately lackluster album sales hammered this message home. "I came face to face with the fact that this was not what people wanted from me. I began finding my direction . . . when I decided to keep 'That's What Love Is All About' for myself. . . . A year earlier I would have sent it to James Ingram."

Michael and his manager, Louis Levin, joke that he owes his success to selfishness, but the best kind. "I didn't really find my niche until I decided to start keeping my ballads and moved away from the edgy, heavier side of Michael Bolton," admits the singer.

(Chuck Pulin/Star File)

"I still have edge in my [live] set but I really feel I've found my stride. . . . I want my songs to be around in twenty years."

If shifting to ballads seems obvious in retrospect, that's because hindsight overlooks the psychological stress involved when a performer changes directions. Bolton was savvy enough to realize he'd gain new fans at the expense of old supporters. Though fame's always been one of Michael's top goals, he spent years singing to and for a predominantly male audience. Would he be considered a traitor who sold out? Did he have the guts to risk it?

Michael told *Us* magazine, "It was a big crisis for me. When you have ballad hits . . . the theme is emotional. And there's a heavy price to pay. You lose a great deal of the male support that would be there and respect you for your voice but who can't deal with the subject matter. So you lose your male audience, and you incur the wrath of the critics. But the success has a way of reassuring you that what you're doing is right."

Bolton's album fulfilled his high expectations: "*The Hunger* kind of put me on the map." It features a huge supporting cast—multiple producers, musicians, co-writers, and guest performers lent support. The result is a nine-cut transition piece that starts familiarly with hard-edged rock before finding the golden groove, devoting itself entirely to ballads in classic Bolton style.

Even the cover photo marks a departure. It's a moody, soft-focus sepia-tone shot that makes Michael seem about twenty years old, not to mention awfully cute and vulnerable. The back cover photo reverts to type with a typical full-frontal shot of Michael glaring into the lens, working his cheekbones for all they're worth. He's artfully backlit so a halo surrounds that curly mane.

Keith Diamond, who has collaborated with singers as different as Billy Ocean and Mick Jagger, produced four cuts on *The Hunger*. Another song was produced by Susan Hamilton. The remaining four were produced by Jonathan Cain, who frequently worked with the rock ensemble Journey. Indeed, Neal Schon, Randy Jackson, and Mike Baird—all from Journey—play on *The Hunger*.

The album was recorded in studios around California and the tracks subsequently brought to New York for mixing. With the exception of "Dock of the Bay," every song is a Bolton co-composition, penned with collaborators Jonathan Cain, Martin Briley, Keith Diamond, Diane Warren, Eric Kaz, Bob Halligan, Jr., and Neal Schon.

In a long list of thanks, Michael again pays special tribute to his family: Maureen, Isa, Holly, and Taryn. He offers "deepest gratitude to Mickey Eichner, Joe McEwen, and Al Teller, who showed their faith and belief." These are the Columbia executives who kept talking about "the next album," and convinced Michael it was time to record his ballads. Among the other thank yous, several names stand out. Bolton thanks his mom, sister and brother, pays tribute to Sally's Pizza ("still the best"), and Joyce Logan, the childhood friend who launched his fan club and continues running it nine years later.

Initially *The Hunger* sounds like more of the same. Cuts one and four, "Hot Love" and "Gina," sound like outtakes from Bolton's hard-rocking days. Then the album magically springs to life. On track three Bolton lets loose with an impassioned—but not *overly* impassioned—version of "Dock of the Bay," the immortal Otis Redding tune. The raw intensity of Bolton's voice evokes his early 70s solo efforts, so heavily influenced by the blues. There's a grittiness here that's often missing from his more polished work. He sings it like he means it and hits the target squarely.

From this line of demarcation the album sustains high emotional intensity, focusing on the kind of power ballads that are now Bolton's trademark but which must have startled fans expecting a collection of driving rockers.

"That's What Love Is All About," which critic Robert K. Oermann calls a "gut-wrenching song," was the first single. Bolton doesn't miss an opportunity to twist the knife vocally, and audiences ate it up. The song's message that love endures through good times and bad made "That's What Love Is All About" an instant favorite with brides and a staple at weddings.

But it took the album's second single, the can't-miss "Dock of the Bay," to transform this seasoned veteran into an overnight singing sensation. Did Bolton resent fate's quirkiness, given his stature as a sought-after songwriter? No. A great song is a great song, no matter who writes it. He told Oermann, "It's an irony, but it's far from cruel. After all, it's a big international hit. It's opened the Big Door for me." "Dock" rose high on the charts and Bolton was asked to perform on "Showtime at the Apollo."

That appearance led to one of his greatest career triumphs: "Zelma Redding was watching and . . . called my manager and said that she cried . . . that it was the best version since her husband's. I have worked so hard for success in this business, and then to have a moment like that was so gratifying that it cut deeper than record sales!" Today Michael keeps a framed copy of Zelma's congratulatory letter displayed in his home office. Zelma wrote that Michael's performance "reminded me so much of my husband . . . I am honored that [Michael] chose to record it."

(Wasyluk)

Praise from Zelma and "Dock" co-writer Steve Cropper helped cut the sting of critics who insisted it was blasphemy for anyone—especially a white boy—to assay Redding's hit. Bolton defended himself. "Some radio people felt it was a sacrilege to re-record a song which so strongly reminds people of a certain time in their lives. There's something in 'Dock,' whether people know it or not, that relates to the human condition and affects people of all ages. So you've got to make sure you nail it with the same sentiment and conviction—otherwise you catch all hell."

As his career gained momentum, Bolton went high-profile. In October of 1987 Michael joined a host of American songwriters for an exciting trip to the Soviet Union, where they collaborated with Russian writers. Other tunesmiths on the trip included Barry Mann ("You've Lost That Loving Feeling"), Diane Warren ("Time, Love & Tenderness"), Desmond Child ("What It Takes"), Cyndi Lauper ("True Colors"), Holly Knight, Brenda Russell ("Piano in the Dark"), Frannie Golde ("Here I Go Falling in Love Again"), Tom Kelly, and Billy Steinberg.

During the following summer Bolton toured as an opening act for Heart, the Seattle-based band fronted by Ann and Nancy Wilson. Between shows he promoted *The Hunger* with countless radio, print, and television interviews, often struggling out of bed

60

before dawn to appear on morning news shows. After "Dock," three more singles came off the album: "Wait on Love," "Walk Away" (a dark paean to the death of an illicit love), and "Gina."

Despite the attention newly focused on his singing, Bolton remained active as a writer, too. He wrote and produced Cher's hit "I Found Someone" for her 1988 comeback album. Indeed, he gets a lot of credit for restoring her status as a top-ranked pop diva after several years devoted to acting. Certainly Cher recognized his contribution. When she returned to the studio for 1989's *Heart of Stone* Cher wanted Bolton on hand.

Yet Bolton hesitated about his level of involvement. He doesn't like being penned in and had reached a tricky point, trying to balance his career options. He told an interviewer, "I'm only gonna do three or four songs. I don't enjoy spending all that time in the recording studio. I enjoy performing too much. . . . One of the things I enjoy most is performing the songs I've written. . . . I've gotta do this. The thought has never entered my mind to give up performing."

True to his word, Bolton wrote and produced just three tracks, "You Wouldn't Know Love," "Still in Love With You," and "Starting Over." In her playful liner notes Cher nicknames everyone, and teasingly thanks "Michael 'How's my hair?' Bolton" for his help.

Alanna Nash, a critic for *Stereo Review*, gave Bolton high marks as a producer when reviewing *Heart of Stone*. "[Bolton] insists on a cleaner, less cluttered instrumental approach and coaxes a more three dimensional, soulful delivery from her, as in 'You Wouldn't Know Love.' "

Building strength on strength, Michael came out with *Soul Provider* in June of 1989. Again, the album was deliberately crafted and marketed to showcase his soulful side and a voice Robert K. Oermann praised with high marks: "He's blessed with a remarkable vocal instrument, full of dark bluesy shades and fiery rock tones. In short, he was born to sing."

Writer Michael Angeli beautifully described Bolton's voice as "a remarkable instrument . . . his vocal cords pump iron. A range close to three octaves gives him the baritone access of Bill Medley on the low end and the lilt of Smokey Robinson on the top, a tenor rich in minerals with an edge of decay."

If *The Hunger* represented Bolton's struggle to locate his niche as a performer, *Soul Provider* "was like finding the bull's-eye and nailing it dead center." Bolton calls this the big "explosion." The album went platinum four times over, dished up five hit singles, and garnered him two Grammy nominations.

As usual, Bolton surrounded himself with talent. Songwriting assistance came via Andrew Goldmark, Diane Warren, Doug James, Desmond Child, Eric Kaz, and Barry Mann. The songs are: "Soul Provider"; "Georgia on My Mind" (by Hogey Carmichael and S. Gorrell); "It's Only My Heart"; "How Am I Supposed to Live Without You"; "How Can We Be Lovers"; "You Wouldn't Know Love"; "When I'm Back on My Feet Again"; "From Now On" (sung with Suzie Benson); "Love Cuts Deep"; and "Stand Up for Love."

Like *The Hunger*, this album was recorded in California with different producers, including Peter Bunetta, Rick Chudacoff, Bolton, Susan Hamilton, Michael Omartian, Desmond Child, and Guy Roche. Singer Richard Marx adds background vocals to one cut and Kenny G plays saxophone on several others.

More than its forerunners, *Soul Provider* concentrates on love's problems, peering into the darkness and shadows. There's a great atmosphere of loss here, and Bolton's full-throttle singing pounds home the intense sense of desperation. It's an emotional album. His version of "How Am I Supposed to Live Without You" may be Bolton's ultimate heartwrencher, relying on the crying hitch in his voice to reel in buckets of tears.

This full-throttle delivery repeats on cut after cut. "How Can We Be Lovers" *starts* with the blast-furnace chorus and escalates into the kind of fever pitch intensity that draws him critical fire. His version of Warren's "When I'm Back on My Feet Again" relies on the same all-out tactics to emphasize her lyrics about nearly plunging over the edge but finding redemption just in time.

Interestingly, Bolton and Cher simultaneously released "You Wouldn't Know Love" in 1989. He produced both tracks to be virtually identical, except that Cher's voice is deeper and angrier. They even shared some backup singers, so it's tempting to wonder if Bolton wandered from studio to studio with pre-recorded tracks, slotting them in when needed.

Soul Provider sold more than seven million copies and still rode the charts as this book went to press. Bolton attributed the album's staying power to word of mouth. He told *Billboard*, "My fans tell a lot of people about [*Soul Provider*]. They play it in their cars for friends and people say, 'What *is* this?'—and that's why it keeps going and the momentum is there after almost two years."

The killer combination of Bolton's passionate vocals and Kenny G.'s sax solo on "How Am I Supposed to Live Without You" sent the tune back to Number One six years after Laura Branigan first made it a hit. It stayed on top for three weeks. Michael followed it with his version of Ray Charles's anthem, "Georgia on

My Mind," which succeeded on both the Top 40 and Hot Black Singles charts.

"How Can We Be Lovers" was also a hit. This song addresses one of Bolton's favorite themes: "There's this concept, men and women can't be close friends because we're so different. But in reality, the people I see having healthy relationships, those are people that you can see they're really, really close friends. And it's a simple thing, because you don't cheat on your friend, you don't do things that you think could potentially hurt your friend, you don't deprive your friend.

"I don't think you're missing out on anything that way. I'm convinced . . . that it's the key to a great long relationship. A man and a woman becoming best friends . . . and getting all the other great stuff that comes with it."

Soul Provider earned a mixed review from Alanna Nash, who called the vocals disturbing. "He sings in a forced, unnatural rasp like Joe Cocker and Michael McDonald, or at least in a style that simply does not come readily to a grown-up white boy. As a result you fear that his voice will break at any instant." Once past that terror, she found his range occasionally "powerful and spellbinding . . . but his bigger gift is songwriting." Even so, she cautioned, Bolton tunes veer dangerously toward sentimentality and overwrought angst.

Bolton accompanied the album with a thirty-minute, three-video compilation on SMV (Sony Music Video Enterprises). *Soul Provider: The Videos* features clips for "How Am I Supposed to Live Without You," "How Can We Be Lovers," and "Soul Provider." The collection went platinum during the summer of 1990.

Dressed in a jazzy black and white shirt and a dark jacket, Michael introduces each video and chats easily about his career as if the viewer were an old friend. "Success is great," he says with a beaming smile. "It keeps me charged up. But it's not the way I pictured it ten years ago."

When it's time to make videos, admitted Michael, he usually had a distinct look and message in mind but welcomed advice from the technical team. The final images come from intensive brainstorming and planning sessions with his record label, plus mid-shoot improvisation.

" 'Soul Provider' feels like an old fashioned cafe song," said Michael. To capture that gentle, nostalgic mood, the video's sepia and color-suffused images shift between Bolton singing into an old-time microphone and a deserted beach where a lovely brunette lady sways to the music.

For "How Am I Supposed To Live Without You" Bolton and Columbia kept asking themselves, Performance or concept? "Here it was important for me to get the general feel of the song across. I wanted something soft, sensual, and emotional." They chose concept, and wound up with a very sexy video. As it opens Michael is leaving an apartment after a shattered romance. The video backtracks, showing how matters evolved to this sad point as Michael and a gorgeous blond find and then lose one another.

Finally, "How Can We Be Lovers" alternates high-energy shots of Bolton and his band belting out the tune with tableaux of Michael and a woman at various crucial relationship points—fighting, kissing, talking, not talking. There's even a glimpse of Bolton's naked torso as he lies in bed under a sheet. Concept shots are filmed in black-and-white, the performance in vivid color.

By the end of 1989 awards were pouring in. That year Bolton won a New York Music Award for Best Male R&B Artist. Then "How Am I Supposed to Live Without You" earned him his first Grammy nomination *and* win as Best R&B Male Artist. Accepting his Grammy, Bolton laughed that his wasn't much of an overnight success. "More like 3,642 nights." That was a rare flash of humor, since Bolton, who can joke about most things, is notorious for being "dead serious when it comes to my career."

He broke records by walking off with four more New York Music Awards in 1990—the only artist to win that many in a single year, garnering trophies for Artist of the Year, Best Male R&B Artist, Best Male Pop Vocalist, and Best Pop Album, for *Soul Provider*. "How Am I Supposed to Live Without You" was BMI's Song of the Year. In 1991 Michael was nominated for a second Grammy for his version of "Georgia On My Mind," still from the *Soul Provider* collection.

Bolton and Kenny G performed "How Am I Supposed to Live Without You" on the 1990 Grammy telecast and brought an audience of industry insiders to its feet cheering enthusiastically. The duo took to the road for a sixty-city summer tour that crossed America, playing to sold-out audiences. The tour won awards from both *Performance* and *Pollstar* magazines as "Most Creative Package." Manager Louis Levin jokes, "We went from opening for Ozzy Osbourne, literally, to having the tour of the year in 1990 with Kenny G."

Kenny G is a Seattle born and based saxophone player who also happens to be a qualified accountant. Many feel he plays like a CPA, lacking the fire and depth of a true jazzman. England's *Q*

MICHAEL

BOLTON

(Ernst Weber, Jr.)

(Ernst Weber, Jr.)

In 1991

In 1989

KIIS-FM sponsored the "Time, Glove and Tenderness" tour at the West Wilshire Park in West Hollywood

(Bob Scott/Celebrity Photo)

(Scott Downie/Celebrity Photo)

With Nicolette Sheridan at the Carousel of Hope Ball held at the Beverly Hilton Hotel, Los Angeles, October 2, 1992

Kenny G and Michael at Jones Beach in New York City, where they performed together

magazine calls his work "jazz for people who like the idea but aren't too keen on the music." He and Michael are close friends who joke that they're "twin sons of different mothers." In addition to Kenny's work on Michael's albums, Bolton sings "Don't Make Me Wait For Love" on *Kenny G Live*.

Bolton opened these summer shows; he wouldn't headline until the *Time, Love & Tenderness* tour. During Michael's set Kenny G joined him for a duet on "Georgia." The high point of each evening came during their high-intensity pairing on "How Am I Supposed to Live Without You," a show-stopping finale that left fans breathless.

Seeing Bolton and Kenny G in action, it's clear how much this team enjoys working together. On Bolton's NBC special, Kenny praised his friend lavishly: "When Michael and I perform together in front of an audience, there's this magic that happens that I've never experienced before and it's far greater than the sum of the individual parts. It is awesome. When we look at each other and the audience is out there, there's this knowing look between us where we know something's happening that's really magical. Those moments I cherish, and I'm so glad that I've been able to experience it."

Not everyone was enthusiastic about this match. Critics and fans sheared off to opposite poles. Reviewing a performance at the Saratoga Performing Arts Center, *Billboard*'s Michael Eck damned Bolton *and* Kenny G equally: "Their music seemed made of pyrite—the duo had all the right moves but not quite the right stuff." Calling Michael stiff and melodramatic, he said the performers "ooze craft, not soul."

In the *Los Angeles Times* Don Heckman moaned that the show was overlong, overblown, and overly repetitious. He called Bolton's "blue-eyed soul style . . . an acquired taste, which requires almost complete ignorance of the more fruitful sources upon which it is based."

Bolton fared no better with the critic from San Francisco. Joel Selvin's *San Francisco Chronicle* review complained, "There's a big difference between having a voice and being able to sing." He nicknamed the Bolton/Kenny G double bill "Twin Beaks," echoing the sentiment that vocal gyrations can't disguise a severe lack of soul. Selvin remarked that the capacity crowd consisted almost entirely of sex-crazed women.

He also printed an unflattering story, claiming Bolton told the audience he objected to Streisand recording "We're Not Makin' Love Anymore" for her 1989 album *A Collection: Greatest Hits*

...*And More*. According to Selvin, Bolton arrogantly claimed, "But what could I do? She was bigger than me . . . back then." This directly contradicts Michael's testimony on television, where he said, "I felt like it was a great honor having Barbra Streisand record the song first." It seems unlikely anyone would object to Streisand choosing to record one of their songs. Perhaps this was an example of that slippery Bolton humor mistaken for seriousness as it flew over the reviewer's head. In any event, Michael never regrets giving away a song because it's always possible to go back and make your own recording later.

With *Soul Provider* Michael altered destiny. He was now an official heartthrob and unqualified popular success. But from a critical standpoint, life would never be rosy again. If Bolton had lost his male audience, he lost the reviewers along with them. From here on in it was love him or leave him. No one occupied the middle ground.

(Todd Kaplan/Star File)

6 Tell Me How You Feel

Michael came in off the road and headed straight for the studio, where he put together his fifth Columbia album, 1991's *Time, Love & Tenderness*. Columbia pre-released "Love Is a Wonderful Thing," which was a radio hit for three months prior to the album's arrival. In April the album shot to Number One after just three weeks. Additional singles flew off in rapid succession. This didn't surprise Bolton; he counted on this collection to chart time and again. "I'm really looking forward to when we get to the fourth and fifth singles on this record. People are going to say, 'Whoa—there's *more*?'" He wasn't disappointed.

This album was produced by Walter Afanasieff with Bolton and was predominantly recorded at Plant Studios in Sausalito, California. Bolton co-wrote eight of the ten songs: "Love Is a Wonderful Thing," "Missing You Now," "Forever Isn't Long Enough," "Now That I Found You," "We're Not Makin' Love Anymore," "New Love," "Save Me," and "Steel Bars." "Time, Love & Tenderness" is a Diane Warren composition. Michael also covered the Percy Sledge hit "When a Man Loves a Woman," credited to C. Lewis and A. Wright.

Bolton loves collaborating on new material because it keeps songwriting exciting, constantly exposing him to fresh approaches. As usual he had an all-star cast of co-authors. In addition to proven chartbusters Diane Warren, Andrew Goldmark,

Desmond Child and Walter Afanasieff, Bolton penned a hit with Bob Dylan. Yes, *that* Bob Dylan.

How did this startling union come about? Actually Dylan requested it. Michael told the *Detroit News* he got a bolt-from-the-blue call from an employee of the legendary performer requesting that he drive up to Dylan's mountaintop home. "I'd written lyrics I thought were Dylanesque. I've never had the confidence of delivering them. I was getting nervous as I was driving up there. . . . Can I write lyrics with Bob Dylan in the same room?

"I picked up an acoustic guitar and played some ideas that I thought felt like Bob Dylan in the 90s. Then he'd come up with a line. Then I'd sing another line. We worked a few hours. The last line and a half he sent me two days before I did the final vocal. I

(Wasyluk)

hope he's happy with it. I am." Of all his compositions, Bolton says "Steel Bars" was the quickest to write.

"Steel Bars" sounds nothing like Dylan and everything like pure Bolton product, especially with its lush chorus driven by the efforts of six bellowing backup vocalists. Michael admitted to *Billboard*, "It was an honor for me. I wanted to write something that

Circa 1984

(Larry Busacca/Retna)

musically would feel that Dylan was in it that would be comfortable for me to sing . . . and not feel like *exactly* what Dylan would do on a Michael Bolton record. As it turns out, it's kind of like 'Dylan meets Bolton-Jovi' or something. It's got this big hook."

The saga took a humorous spin by the time Michael chatted to Michael Angeli from *Esquire* and started really letting his hair down. Apparently Dylan wrestled mightily with some troublesome lyrics. "He comes in, says something like, 'I could not bear what would materialize, but you, so ready to etherealize.' I said, 'Gee, I don't know, Bob. That's kind of a lot of syllables for me.' He shrugged and said, 'Yeah, I guess so,' and went back out," said Bolton, adding, "I think Bob respects my voice; I don't know if Bob really is interested in the kind of music that I've had success with." Maybe Dylan was interested in potential revenue more than the genre—it's been years since he's broken the *succes d'estime* mold with a Top Ten single. And "Steel Bars" was a huge hit.

Another notable pairing is Bolton's singing duet with Patti Labelle for a mega-decibel version of "We're Not Makin' Love Anymore." On June 3, they sang it live at the Dorothy Chandler Pavilion for an all-star benefit on behalf of the Los Angeles County Department of Children's Services. The duo reprised their performance in a high energy appearance during Motown's Thirtieth Anniversary Special.

Bolton officially kicked off his Time, Love & Tenderness Tour in July and went on to play more than 150 shows in the United States, Canada, and Europe. He traveled with a five-piece band, three female backup singers, plus a collection of roadies, technicians, and security personnel. All told, Bolton employs upwards of fifty people when he's on the road. The sellout tour—it's estimated Bolton entertained more than 1.5 million—like the album, delighted Michael's fans. *Both* failed to make critics happy.

Only *L.A.Times* reviewer Dennis Hunt praised *Time, Love & Tenderness*, calling it Bolton's best to date: "Bolton virtually owns the romantic pop R&B ballad turf." Hunt reckoned Michael was doing a public service, bringing R&B to an audience who wouldn't explore it any other way.

People called the collection "solid but overproduced." Geoffrey Himes, of the *Washington Post*, also thought it too commercial. "You can't substitute effort for emotion. . . . Even a real soul singer couldn't top Percy Sledge's classic 1966 performance of ["When a Man Loves a Woman"], so what was Bolton thinking of?"

Newsday's John Leland dismissed Michael as a Neil Diamond for the 90s, a "guy with funny hair who croons torch songs for lite-FM." Leland speculated that Bolton's reliance on classics is an attempt to prove his credentials, a proof that fails because Bolton "punishes" the songs, singing without subtlety. "He's an all-purpose love man, armed with a homily for every occasion. . . . Bolton gives pillow talk at F-16 volume. He's a chronicler of the most ordinary love, but that's probably part of his appeal. He gets sweaty rather than clever."

Bolton violently disagrees with those who say he's not vocally or spiritually equipped to sing soul. Admittedly, early in his career he risked permanent physical damage by singing incorrectly, but he has since learned what's what. "I'd like to feel that I've learned the important things about singing. Singing soul is singing from your soul. If you can't get there, then it's just going to sound like pseudo-soul, like you're trying. And I hear white singers and black singers who sound that way. And I can tell the difference between when you're trying and when you're there. I just never want to hear me trying."

At every venue Michael was joined by a local church choir to sing background vocals on "Time, Love & Tenderness" and "When I'm Back on My Feet Again." Yet it's a wonder anyone could hear them. Charles M. Young described the pandemonium typical of a Bolton gig: "Perfume is the odor of the hour. When the

(Barry King/Gamma Liaison)

lights go down, this middle-class multitude erupts into a terrifying howl . . . and an eerie groan of lust and yearning unheard since the Maenads were dismembering male witnesses to their Dionysian rituals in ancient Greece." Another writer marveled: "Bolton was performing amid a seemingly incessant torrent of lusty howls and shrieks from the predominantly female crowd."

Backstage Michael pokes fun at his image, joking that he could start his own lingerie store and marveling at all the peculiar gifts fans send him. But once he hits the stage, Bolton's a total professional. He tries not to acknowledge catcalls, though he sometimes removes his jacket when the roaring's too intense. "If women find me attractive and want to scream, throw stuff at me, or bring flowers, that's great," he philosophizes, but "I just don't want to be perceived as remotely in some way like—who are those guys?—the Chippendales."

To avoid beefcake comparisons, he struggles to elevate the tone. Between songs he'll describe how he came to write a particular lyric, or he'll introduce a tune by dropping the name of a famous artist who covered it first. While Bolton's onstage staying cool, security staffers and paramedics working his concerts have their hands full. Women faint and suffer seizures. One very pregnant woman hollered until her water broke!

Bolton is not above exploiting the excitement he causes. The rock and roll equivalent of sticking your head in the lion's mouth is diving into the audience. Bolton performs a variation on this feat by entering the audience to sing "Georgia on My Mind." This choreographed set piece originated during the 1990 tour and became a well-known treat for diehard fans.

First, Bolton excuses himself from the stage, saying he's off to "slip into something more comfortable." After a fifteen-minute lull and costume change he reappears at the back of the auditorium crooning the ballad and moving through the crowd, heavily guarded by what writer Michael Angeli termed "a flying wedge of brawn." Bodyguards create a circle protecting Bolton, who sings "with a bizarre sense of false intimacy, as if you decided to serenade your girlfriend from inside a shark cage."

Women who know the score line up along Bolton's parade route to bombard him with affection. *They're* not bashful, but Michael's security team *is*. These bouncers are quite adept at fighting off other men but hesitate when women are involved. Trouble is, says Michael, "Those women have *nails*!" Sometimes they covet body parts, trying to take home an ear or hank of hair instead of a souvenir tee shirt. Once, Michael regained the stage and declared, "Some of the women out there, they're dressed like ladies, but they're animals!"

Mike Joyce, covering a Bolton show for the *Washington Post*, called it a "dramatically paced crowd pleaser." Despite this professionalism, Joyce found Bolton's all-out delivery relentless. He wasn't paying a compliment when he wrote, "Bolton has never met (or written) a song he couldn't turn into a mini-rock opera."

In Costa Mesa, California, Bolton drew 15,000 to the Pacific Amphitheater. Critic Mike Boehm came away impressed by Bolton's singing and range but like his colleague, wondered if it wasn't all a bit too much. "Bolton may be the Charles Atlas of singers, but you can't swing freely if you're musclebound. And you can't capture the ebb and flow of feelings if you're always trying to belt a tune out of the park." Boehm had little tolerance for Bolton's material, calling it "pablum" based on banalities. It's

The Five Tops

as if, he wrote, Bolton believed "imagination were a crime and cliché a commandment."

Reviewing a show at Manhattan's Paramount Theater, *New York Times* critic Karen Schoemer distilled the essence of Bolton's popularity. "[He] knows how to make every woman in the audience feel special. . . His voice never, ever lets up. He emotes 100 percent of the time. The fantasy he seems to inhabit gratefully never has a chance to dissipate."

Joel Selvin, whose earlier review displayed a rabid distaste for Bolton, caught a concert at the Shoreline Amphitheater. Rather, he *endured* it, complaining that the two-hour-plus show felt eons longer. According to Selvin, when Bolton contorted his face in emotion it looked "like he was trying to pass a difficult bowel movement. . . . [He's] a bogus schlockmeister, heavy on romantic paeans, who left thousands of quivering custards in his wake at Shoreline."

Given such stinging personal criticism, it's no wonder Bolton despises critics. "The most offensive thing . . . is that you see the critic is not really knowledgeable enough about music to be making the kind of criticisms he is. . . . He doesn't get it—and yet he is allowed and has the power to do a critique on your music. . . . And when someone doesn't get it, doesn't understand what

(Allen/Liaison)

you're all about . . . there's a certain amount of injustice in it that is difficult to just write off."

Time, Love & Tenderness, like all of Bolton's work, examines love: love that makes you smile when it's raining, love as a trial and a test, love so strong eternity won't be long enough to play it out.

Together with *Soul Provider*, *Time, Love & Tenderness* proves Michael Bolton has perfected the musical equivalent of a romance novel. That's *not* damning praise. To borrow from Michael Jackson, Bolton's not like other boys. Hard or soft-edged, Bolton songs never focus on one night stands, present women as a collection of body parts, or explicitly describe sex acts. Like most Pisceans, Bolton's a bred-in-the-bone romantic. "No Pisces man is ever short of romance," writes astrologer Linda Goodman. "They fairly breathe it."

Charles M. Young pointed out: "[Bolton] crafts lyrics that reflect none of the paranoid misogyny that has dented heavy metal and rap. . . . He doesn't portray himself as a wounded little boy. He doesn't distance himself with irony or jokes. He portrays himself as a mature man who wants his relationship to work and is willing to talk about his feelings and whatever might be wrong."

Bolton's songs describe relationships that include sex but aren't defined by it. Even "We're Not Makin' Love Anymore" isn't about sex, it's about the difference between fornication and sensual, tender passion that's an expression of emotional intimacy.

Romance novelists consider sex an integral part of character and plot development, not mere titillation or diversion. Though quite graphic, these novels never objectify women or disregard female pleasure. Though formulaic (as are screenplays), they're tough to write properly. If you disagree, try it. Few insist romance novels are literature, but they're an example of sturdy craftsmanship and a lucrative form of entertainment for their creators and vendors.

In Bolton's musical universe women are highly valued. Woman holds the power to hurt or heal. She's his support in a harsh world. He sings about long-term relationships experiencing ups and downs but surviving because both partners stick with it, working out the rough patches, reveling in the ecstasy. Bolton songs, like romance novels, rely on stock formulas, but the challenge stands: Try knocking out a hit song over the weekend.

Viewed in this light, it's not surprising that Bolton is a household name. Women buy millions of romance novels annually. True devotees often devour one per day. In Michael Bolton the

romantically inclined have found a perfect musical complement to their favorite books. He even looks a bit like Fabio, the cover-boy-turned-author who makes hearts throb from coast to coast.

One *People* reader expressed it nicely in her letter to the editor: "I've spent a lot of time in the dark with Michael Bolton's music, and I bet you that the critics who carp about his 'whine' are men. Women translate that 'whine' to mean passion and romance. I know women who have only Michael's music to remind them that passion and romance still exist"—Rose Ferguson, Metarie, Louisiana.

It's also not shocking that so many men—formerly fans—despise Bolton. They've been left out *and* challenged. It's trendy nowadays to recognize that men and women speak different languages and generally miscommunicate. Bolton's bilingual. That, he speculates, "makes men jealous. They can't deal with women relating to you."

Michael considers himself a prototype for the new 90s man, someone who successfully blends strength and sensitivity. He's

78

fulfilling the promise of enlightenment that seemed a certainty for a brief moment in the 80s before the backlash of the men's movement.

Bolton says: "When [women] hear a *man* expressing those feelings, they wish the one in their life would be just as open. It never ceases to disappoint me that so many women are stuck in a relationship rut because of a lack of real communication. So many women settle for abusive relationships because they feel they're not going to do any better if they leave. . . . Macho guys might feel threatened by me.

It's difficult to get a man on your side if his wife or girlfriend is talking about you all the time. He doesn't know what she needs, and she can't explain it other than saying, 'Why can't you be more like Michael Bolton?' *I* couldn't handle that. But I think what the woman wants is just for the guy to express his feelings . . . and that's what I try to get across in my songs. It comes to down to communication, to friendship. You have to respect the woman in your life as you would your best friend. A lot of men, because of the way we're raised, don't understand that."

Men who confront and are reconciled to their vulnerability, who merge their male and female natures, develop a rare kind of charisma. Any Bolton fan will tell you he's got that in spades. So how did Bolton make peace with his warring sides? The trick is, he doesn't see them as antagonists. "Expressing vulnerability—expressing weakness that really does exist—is not about showing weakness, it's showing strength. It's showing the courage to deal with your feelings, to deal with an area that you're not extremely knowledgeable about, but it's honesty. Expressing your feelings is really important."

He echoes these sentiments frequently, telling *Billboard:* "I think my success . . . comes from moving people emotionally. My music, even the up-tempo stuff, is emotionally driven and the content frightens men. Guys don't want to deal with that kind of emotional expression . . . I think that's what women love about my music—and I think that's how they perceive me: as someone who says things that they would like to hear a man express, but with conviction and strength."

Award-winning songwriter Diane Warren, who's known Michael privately and professionally for years, agrees that this is the key to his appeal. "When a man is that vulnerable and sings something that tender, women love that. They melt."

On the downside, we've already seen that Michael fears his music will be overlooked—and with good reason. I'm not just another pretty face, he protests. "I don't want my music to become a background element to the sex-symbol hysteria. . . . Selling sensitivity can be abrasive, not just to those who don't share the sentiments," adds Bolton, "but to the performer who sees himself potentially cheapened. It's like walking into a TV store, seeing a hundred pictures of Timmy crying about Lassie."

Yet with panties flying and women grabbing at him, even Bolton has to admit his concerts are often demented events. One woman boasted she had fourteen orgasms during a concert and consequently didn't need to see her husband for six months!

It's supremely ironic, then, that as Bolton recorded *Time, Love & Tenderness* he was in the throes of an extremely messy divorce ending his fifteen-year marriage. "At the high point of my life and my career I had people calling to congratulate me, and on the other phone it's lawyers calling about depositions," he said. "It was very difficult going in and singing 'Love Is a Wonderful Thing' in some of the darker moments of the divorce. It really digs deep, especially when you've invested a lot of years."

Despite his personal tribulations, Michael classified *Time, Love & Tenderness* as an extremely upbeat album. "Some records have personal problems all over them, somebody's self-absorption, self-indulgence. . . . This is a positive time for me, and my music for this album reflects a new chapter in my life." This is partially because the protracted legal wrangling had been going on for years. By the time this album was ready Michael was a free man. He deliberately avoided songs that would be construed as autobiographical, preferring to look ahead rather than plow old turf.

Fans seeking Bolton's darkest emotions do better spinning *Soul Provider*, which was probably composed and recorded when Michael and Maureen decided to split. It's certainly more pessimistic than *Time, Love & Tenderness*. Instead of singing that love's wonderful, Bolton sings about a woman who doesn't know what love is. He sings about being down and out but determined to pick himself up and start over. He sings about endings more than beginnings or continuations.

What went wrong with the marriage? Bolton doesn't air private grievances publicly. His mom says, "Michael doesn't talk about his feelings. He puts all his emotions into his music." In any event, the terms of his divorce settlement call for silence on both sides. Michael admitted he and Maureen tried counseling but that the situation had deteriorated beyond repair.

There's been speculation in *The Star* that Bolton womanized

his way through the marriage, cheating continuously. The tabloid claimed access to courtroom testimony which alleged Bolton had numerous affairs.

Who knows? When fan club members asked, "What's your favorite animal," Michael answered, "Definitely women!" He's gone on record saying that the divorce wasn't a case of success becoming the other woman. "I've always been career-oriented—it comes with the territory. The fact is, I don't know a lot of people in any walk of life who have been married for more than ten or twelve years." Though Bolton wanted the split, rumor has it he begged Maureen to reconsider and lost control when she began dating.

Not that Bolton stayed home wrapped in a cuddly robe eating ice cream from the carton. Throughout 1989–91 papparazzi snapped him at an endless succession of black tie events, always impeccably dressed, squiring a gorgeous woman. He's dated Brooke Shields, Vanity, Paula Abdul, Julia Roberts, Cindy Garvey, Terri Hatcher, Colleen Morris, and tennis champ Gabriella Sabatini. Bolton acquired a tabloid reputation as a mender of broken hearts because he dated Ivana Trump's rival, Marla Maples, after one of her tiffs with The Donald, and now romances "Knots Landing" star Nicollette Sheridan, who's split from husband Harry Hamlin.

Michael doesn't regret his marriage because it produced three wonderful kids. The hardest part of breaking up was his enforced separation from the girls. "The worst thing about divorce is that you don't hear your kids' voices in the morning. You don't read to them at night," he complained.

Being a weekend dad nearly destroyed him. "There's something instinctively wrong with being a visiting parent," he said. "You get into the mentality where you're living to put the last ten years into the next weekend. I don't know if I was ruining the good times because I was always so concerned about quality time."

Of course life as a super-successful pop star creates additional burdens even as it eases financial dramas. "It's difficult enough being a single parent. It's difficult enough feeling like there's enough of you to go around for your kids. It's worse when you have to travel, not having as much time to relax with the kids is very brutal sometimes."

When they were younger Bolton felt the road was no place for kids. Now the girls occasionally join him if he's stopping somewhere interesting, like New Orleans. Bolton outfits them with special "all-access" backstage passes and assigns a security guard to ensure their safety. At other times he'll bring them along on a fun charity outing, like the VH-1 celebrity ski benefit held in 1990.

Michael waged a successful two-year custody battle. Currently the two youngest girls, Holly and Taryn, live with him full-time at his adjacent Westport homes—one for family, one for work. The eldest, Isa, lives nearby with Maureen. Michael hopes that one day he and Maureen will develop a friendship, but for now there's too much animosity between them.

Bolton realizes kids need both parents and would never stand between Maureen and the girls. "There's no defined obligation about visitation. It's loose. Isa will come when she feels like it, she's here sometimes just seeing her sisters when I'm out of town. And the kids can just pick up the phone and head over to see Mom. . . . It's very open."

Michael allowed Holly and Taryn to be filmed but not interviewed on his television special, begging off with the excuse, "I don't want to drag them into my stuff. . . . I don't want to exploit my kids." Later, when *People* sent Steve Dougherty to Connecticut for an interview, he relented, allowing them to participate.

Michael is an extremely devoted parent, really active, involved, totally hands-on. "My social life in Connecticut is hanging out with my kids. With three girls that means shopping. They don't realize how it makes me feel to be able to say 'yes' to what they want—it's been a long time. . . . For years, I couldn't afford anything, even rent. Now I can do what I want. . . . It's great to be able to say, 'Yes, how about next Wednesday we fly to Disneyworld?' "

Though there's tremendous residual guilt about the years of poverty, Bolton worries about spoiling his daughters and turning them into princesses who don't appreciate the importance of hard work. Like many parents he's easily manipulated by his girls' kisses or tears. Taryn said, "He tries not to spoil us, yet he doesn't like to say no. He's a major pushover. We say, 'Pleeease, Dad!' And he's, like, 'OK!' "

And the Bolton girls "play hardball. I'll be on the phone screaming about business and one of the kids calls saying, 'You know I saw this dress today.' So next I'm talking to a store, giving them my charge card. . . . We were on an island for nine days and they begged me to stay two more. Theirs was a simple, below-the-belt technique: All three climbed on me and began kissing my face saying, 'Please, please, please.' They won."

Joyce Logan, a lifelong friend and president of his fan club, says Michael's "like a lion with cubs when it comes to his kids." When they were young, he revealed, everything seemed threatening. "I wanted to pad all the sharp corners with pillows."

These days the threat's more likely to be sharp-dressed boys. *USA Today* asked if Bolton worried, now that the girls are dating. He said it made a detective out of him. "I might've just come back from Europe, but the second I'm home, it's right into, 'OK, I'm the head of security here.' What can you do? You can tell them everything, but . . . you cannot police them." Later he added, "It's a fine line to walk where you're a friend and at the same time the authority."

Michael jokes that he greets his daughters' dates with a bazooka gun. Actually, he often invites the young couple out to dinner at a restaurant of their choosing so he can get acquainted with the boy. Michael described a typical night out: "The kid's nervous and I try to lighten everything up. I tell them there's a big, deep lake in the back and I'm sure he'll behave like a gentleman [he mimics Don Corleone] with my daughters."

Communication is as critical to good parenting as it is in a love affair, he stresses. He and the girls have a pact to eat dinner together every night, even if he's knee deep in a recording session next door. "At 6:30 . . . Holly calls me up and . . . whatever we're doing in the studio, it waits until after dinner or until the kids are up doing their homework or in bed."

Around the table topics range from school and boys to politics and AIDS. The girls are encouraged to open up. "I want to feel they can tell me anything, and that's a tough one to shoot for—I'm a man and their father. At dinner the floodgates open and they talk about a lot of things that other dads miss out on because they're uncomfortable about it."

Where sex and AIDs are concerned, Bolton says, "It's a little tough because I'm a father, not the mother. The best thing to do is always try and be a friend with your kid so they can feel free to talk to you about anything and you can feel free to talk to them about anything. And it's about caring and staying in communication, making sure that your information's accurate, that everyone knows what's going on."

To nurture intimacy, Bolton flies home between tour dates as often as possible, either weekly or biweekly, and burns up the telephone wires in between these pit stops.

Michael remembers conflicts with his dad because George placed such emphasis on excellence and achievement. Bolton works to show his daughters they're loved unconditionally. He encourages them to "travel their own journey. . . . I don't want them to ever feel that they have to succeed because of me, that they have to be the best at anything because I'm expecting it of them. To me it's more important that the support is there, no matter how they do. No matter what anybody told me, I had to learn my way. And I expect it will be the same case with my girls."

(Frank Micelotta/Retna)

7 Take Me As I Am

As 1991 closed, Michael Bolton joked, "My next album will be called *Stress Is a Wonderful Thing*." What a premonition! Throughout 1992 Michael grew increasingly popular with fans, steadily more loathsome to critics and a cadre of older, black musicians who resented his rise to fame as an interpreter of R&B. Bolton realizes negativity comes with fame; critics don't pick on nobodies. Still, one thing harder than launching a career is keeping it afloat. "The more success you have, the more demanding it is. Like a video game, once you get past the first screen, there are flying saucers with laser missiles shooting at you." The way things are going Bolton could license his story to Nintendo!

Time, Love & Tenderness continued selling steadily and auguries pointed to a terrific year. In January, Michael won two American Music Awards for Favorite Pop/Rock Male Artist and Favorite Pop/Rock Album. The next month he collected a Grammy for his Number One pop/adult contemporary crossover smash "When a Man Loves a Woman." But a few chance remarks backstage escalated into a controversy that neither Michael nor his critics can put to rest.

At the Grammy telecast Bolton performed "When a Man Loves a Woman" with his customary dramatic flair. Minutes later septuagenarian Irving Gordon received an award for "Unforgettable." Accepting it, he wisecracked, "It's nice to be involved with

Michael with Vanity, 1990

(Scott Downie/Celebrity Photo)

With Gabriella Sabatini in New York City

(Magnani/Gamma Liaison)

With Paula Abdul,
1990

(Scott Downie/Celebrity

(Scott Downie/Celebrity Photo)

**With Colleen Morris at the
American Cinema Awards,
1991**

(Scott Downie/Celebrity Photo)

a song that doesn't sound like you have a hernia as you're singing it."

Bolton initially thought this was a random comment, not a personal assault. "He could have been referring to me or he could have been referring to contemporary music," he rationalized. "I'm looking at a guy who is out of touch with reality and is rambling on national TV. . . . But regardless of how inflammatory his statements were, I was also looking at a guy who was probably experiencing the high moment of his musical life. At his age, he might not get another one. So let him have it."

Bolton went on to win the Grammy for "When a Man Loves a Woman." His acceptance speech paid tribute to several people who helped create the record but neglected to mention the song's originator, Percy Sledge. "I certainly didn't mean any disrespect to him. And I wrote a letter immediately to him [saying that]. Everyone knows I've always thought that his was the ultimate version of that song. But when you get up to receive a Grammy, it's very exciting. There were a few people I didn't thank. I tried to rattle off who I could remember. And, of course, the critics are just looking for anything if they hate you."

Even seasoned professionals accustomed to performing live get rattled when they're receiving an award. It's exciting, scary, and unscripted. "When you win a Grammy, tell me what it's like. Until then, shut, up," joked Bolton to one reporter. "You get nervous up there. You don't know what you're saying. I just forgot."

Unfortunately when Michael reached the press room for post-award photos and sound bites, critics were gunning for him. He didn't know they booed throughout his acceptance speech. He did react when a female reporter tactlessly asked, "How do you feel about some of these people? They not only seem to dislike you, they seem to hate you." Talk about letting the wind out of someone's sails. Bolton reeled. "It was such a strong, abrasive thing to say. . . . It just took me by surprise. I'd taken a hundred shots." To add insult to injury, it was Michael's birthday.

Wounded, Bolton bared his fangs. He says getting caught off guard prompted him to say exactly what he felt, and he likened critics to chimps slinging paint at the great masters. "All I basically said was if these guys don't like what I'm doing, that's one thing. But if they're going to be rude and cruel, they can kiss my ass. It was a spontaneous reaction."

Spontaneous, yes, but does he regret the outburst? Sort of: "I regret saying that because I think chimpanzees are a higher life form." Later Michael said, "There were a bunch of guys in the

Michael attended the Twentieth American Music Awards with Nicolette Sheridan

corner who were the rock critics. They looked like a bunch of X-rated movie bit players, the guys who play the bartenders or the dweebs who finally get laid." Naturally they reacted to his slur with more hissing and booing. As Bolton remembers, "They were shocked, as if I was gonna say, 'Oh, gee, we all have our own type of music and hate is natural.'"

Nearly every critic has taken a potshot at Michael over the incident, but he did receive a supportive letter from Michael Greene, president of the National Academy of Recording Arts and Sciences, which bestows the Grammys. Greene wrote, "Whether we like it or not these clowns have a consistent forum to ensure that their opinions get heard day in, day out. We do not."

In a scathing article entitled "Soul Drain," *GQ* columnist Gerri Hirshey went after Bolton hammer and tong. She was home watching the Grammys with Sam Moore, of Sam and Dave fame. When Bolton won, Sam cried, *"How about thanking Percy Sledge, man?"*

Besides the Sledge oversight, Hirshey excoriated Bolton, denigrating his hairstyle ("the distressed shredded wheat do"), his arrangements ("goopy strings, horn vamps and cookie-cutter rhythm tracks . . . enough women dig his crinkle-cut *je ne sais quoi* to make him an easy listening sex god"), and his voice ("the vocal equivalent of matadors painted on black velvet").

Hirshey made an interesting point: that historically, tough economics "brew tepid pop; these surges of musical dweebitude seem to be a reactive if unconscious conservatism." The last such wave swept America in the 1970s, she said, going on to point out that Bolton didn't hit—despite years of trying—until after Black Monday.

In *The New York Times* Sam Moore commented, "[Bolton] certainly gives women what they want, so he's doing something right. . . . I'd like to see Michael on a package tour like we used to do. I'd like to hear Michael go on after Sam Cooke or Jackie Wilson. It would make him a better entertainer, or it would send him to the booby hatch."

Why *do* critics hate Bolton so violently? Bolton's voice doesn't lack strength or beauty, they say, but he employs it poorly. Most commentary slags his hellbent for leather delivery and frequent disregard for modulation. Sam Moore expressed this idea quite well: "I don't hear him working a song like Otis did. You got to build a song from the ground and end at the top of the hill. He tends to start at the top of the hill, and then he has no place to take it."

Critics also resent Bolton's "appropriation" of R&B and his immodest claim that "some of my vocal performances are more soulful than performances by some of the very soulful black singers." Hirshey argues that by calling himself "real," Bolton undercuts an indigenous American art form, selling paste for diamonds, not unlike the Yankee peddlers and their phony nutmegs. Nearly every critic doubts Bolton's sincerity, which is peculiar, given his oft-professed lifelong love of R&B. This *is* Bolton's favorite music.

Noted music writer Dave Marsh finds Bolton's work more akin to an Al Jolson minstrel show than true soul singing. "He can hit the notes in a muscular way, but it's like a student driver oversteering a car. It's . . . a wretched excess of effect—pompous, empty and aggrandizing. . . . And I think he can be knocked for not properly crediting his sources. What did Michael Bolton ever do for Percy Sledge?"

Michael feels critics are jealous, and he has a point. He speculates: "There does seem to be something outside of my work

Spotted at LAX Airport in Los Angeles, 1991

(Bob Scott/Celebrity Photo)

tainting their opinions. Some of the reviews are so cruel, so bitter in their venting, that I'm at a loss for words. I just don't read reviews anymore. There's a Machiavellian theory that a man will hate you if you threaten to take his property or his woman. I have a big following among women because of these emotions that I express . . . If I'm having success without critical support, wouldn't I represent a threat to their self-worth?"

It's also true that nothing infuriates certain critics—and laymen—more than success. They'd rather belong to a secret society of admirers than share their find with the world and see it become public property.

As far as Michael is concerned "Bolton bashing" is another measure of his phenomenal success. "The thing [critics] hate is a feeling of powerlessness. They didn't make me, and they can't break me. . . . People I know in the industry who are really successful, well we look at bitter critics as people who will never achieve anything in their lives. . . . But collectively they can get together and pat each other on the back like little kids: 'Oh, I saw you rip Michael Jackson. Man, you slaughtered him.' "

Though Mojo Nixon penned a ditty called "Michael Bolton Must Die," it's not true that Michael lacks supporters within the industry. Contrary to myth, countless heavyweight talents respect and admire his work. Gladys Knight is a fan, so are Quincy Jones and Liza Minnelli. Zelma Redding and Steve Cropper gave him a rave review. One night in a Manhattan club Michael jammed with Elton John, B. B. King, and Bonnie Raitt. Ray Charles likes him. And Michael reports, "I've had the great joy of having Stevie Wonder tell me I was a great singer; and of having some of the Temptations compliment me, telling me I do Marvin Gaye *right*."

Bolton's also a popular, affable guest on television chat shows. He's been featured many times on "Entertainment Tonight," "Oprah Winfrey," and "Arsenio Hall." He's also appeared on "Saturday Night Live," "CBS This Morning," "Live with Regis and Kathy Lee," and "Tonight." Cable networks from VH-1 to E! Entertainment TV have all run specials on Michael's fascinating career.

As 1992 progressed, Michael was asked to sing the national anthem at a Knicks/Bulls playoff game. It's a tough tune for singers. Michael says, "It's not my favorite song. It's a very unusual choice of notes." Bolton took the gig so he could meet his hero, Woody Allen. Like the fans who worship *him*, Michael went all aquiver: "We shook hands and it was one of the few times that I've been actually speechless."

He sang the anthem again at the All-Star Game and received a wonderful compliment from one of the players. "Charles Barkley came up to me in the locker room. He says, 'You're my favorite singer, you're number one. And you better stay that way.' "

Later in the year Bolton unveiled a new album. *Timeless (The Classics)* pays tribute to the soundtrack of his childhood. With the exception of "White Christmas," every cut is an interpretation of a soul/R&B classic. On the surface *Timeless* wasn't much of a risk; standards albums are traditionally successful. Artists as diverse as Linda Ronstadt, Willie Nelson, and Natalie Cole all boosted their careers with similar releases. *Newsday*'s John Leland noticed old R&B records acquiring "the sheen of pop standards and slipping into the softies niches for which they were never intended. Bolton is among the first major performers to land directly in that easy soul featherbed."

Why *Timeless*? Initially it was envisioned as a filler piece while Bolton concentrated on writing new material. The album and its seventy-seven-city tour filled the coffers, allowing him to retreat without losing the continuity of nonstop radio exposure with songs that are news to his fans. In the liner notes he explained: "While in the process of writing and producing songs for

(A. Berliner/Gamma Liaison)

my next album, I found myself suddenly compelled to record a special classics album and soon became obsessed with this project."

Bolton wasn't trying to play it safe. "The safe thing would have been to keep on doing what I was doing," he commented. More than anyone he realized the aggravation and critical attack likely to ensue. After the barrage of nasty remarks calling him an imposter, releasing *Timeless* was tantamount to painting a bullseye on his back. Of course, with his wicked sense of humor, Michael *may* have done it precisely to piss critics off.

Introducing "Dock of the Bay," he once told an audience, "I want to thank a great artist, Otis Redding. . . . I don't think it matters when a song was written. Sometimes I catch some fire from people who don't like it when I record one of those classics. Some critics have a problem with that, even if you don't. If you wanna hear it, and I wanna sing it, that's the way it's going to be."

He's also said, "If I did what critics wanted I'd be about one-fiftieth as successful as I am. I don't care to do 'alternative' material, and mainstream is an insult to a lot of these people. I have to follow my gut. I'm not saying I do these songs better than the original artists. I'm saying 'I love these songs. If you do, too, great. If not, buy somebody else's record.' "

What started out as a two-month "fun" diversion turned into a major production. Sure, the songs were all in place. But thanks to Michael's "neurotic perfectionism" *Timeless* became as demanding as all his projects. "With this album—just call it delirium or something—I had this idea . . . that I could go in and have fun and make a record. It started out that way, and then I realized, wait a second, this record's gonna be received by millions and millions . . . and are they gonna say, 'Well, I know it's a special project, but does it sound as good to you as the last album?' And I started getting crazy, saying, 'I know I can do this better. We have to go back in.' "

Timeless is dedicated "to the great writers and artists whose performances have made these songs 'the classics' they deserve to be," and was produced by David Foster (who's won or been nominated for twenty-eight Grammy's and worked on Natalie Cole's *Unforgettable*), plus Bolton and Walter Afanasieff.

Bolton wrote: "There are so many great songs, it was difficult to choose, but eventually I put together ten songs that I love and feel passionate about. I hope you appreciate the choices I've made." He chose well. The ten cuts are: Lenny Welch's hit, "Since I Fell for You," by B. Johnson; the Bee Gees' "To Love Somebody"; "Reach Out I'll Be There," recorded by the Four Tops and written by Holland-Dozier-Holland; two Sam Cooke tunes, "You Send Me" and "Bring It on Home to Me"; Lennon and McCartney's chestnut "Yesterday"; M. Williams's "Drift Away," which Dobie Gray made famous; "Knock on Wood" by Eddie Floyd and Steve Cropper; Sam and Dave's hit "Hold On, I'm Coming," by Hayes and Cole Porter; and Irving Berlin's immortal "White Christmas," forever linked to the memory of Bing Crosby's 1942 performance.

Six songs were recorded with a full orchestra, fulfilling a fantasy Bolton cherished since contributing to the Disney compilation *Mad About the Mouse*. "I decided I wanted to cut 'A Dream Is a Wish Your Heart Makes' from *Cinderella* and decided to cut it with an orchestra. I wanted it to feel like something Bing Crosby would've stepped into. And when I started singing with this orchestra, I fell in love with that." Now, instead of adding taped string arrangements separately, Bolton entered the studio along with the musicians.

In *The New York Times*, Charles M. Young gave *Timeless*

94

With Kenny G

mixed marks. He felt Bolton's hyper-emotional style suited tunes like "Since I Fell for You," but destroyed others, such as "White Christmas"—especially contrasted with Crosby's ultra-laid back singing. It's hard to argue with Young's assessment. Bolton delivers Berlin's tune as if it were a lament, belting it out with the dramatic flair of one who doesn't expect he'll live to see another Christmas of *any* hue.

The same might be said of "Yesterday," which begins simply enough with a piano lick, then swells to full orchestration. There's no question that Bolton's voice out-muscles McCartney's, yet his delivery here is enough to propel listeners out of their chairs with a mighty jolt.

He adds muscle to "Bring It on Home," moving it miles away from the sparer Sam Cooke version. Bolton brings in choral voices, giving the song a gospel feeling that's only missing handclapping and swaying to be complete.

If "Knock on Wood" sounds like Michael's audition for a Vegas floor show, his charming version of "Since I Fell for You" is smooth and tasty. "Reach Out" recreates the verve of the perky original version and features background vocals by the fabulous Four Tops, who made this great number a hit. Finally, Bolton's version of "You Send Me" fascinates; all the characteristic rough edges have been smoothed out of his voice. It's a great showcase for his talent, and a rare opportunity to hear him tackle falsetto trills.

Bolton toured with this album and as usual critics threw tomatoes. John Burnes, writing for the *St. Louis Post Dispatch*, griped, "Every song got the same delivery; Bolton started straightforward, wailed a bit, waited out an overlong coda, then went on to the next song."

Bolton arrived at the Hollywood Bowl mid-July. On hand were more than 16,000 rabid supporters and one unamused (but much-read) critic, Robert Hilburn, who titled his review: "5 Million Fans *Can* Be Wrong!" Hilburn loaded his review with adjectives: "overwrought, bombastic, melodramatic, ham-fisted, strained, gross, corny. . . . Face it, the guy's the sledgehammer of pop." The only compliment he could muster addressed Michael's manners; he said Bolton was "gracious" to the audience.

Bolton consulted the dictionary after this review and decided he could live with the criticism. "One of the definitions of overwrought is impassioned. . . . I'm a passionate person and I put it into my music. And if they don't like it, they've gotta go somewhere else." Frequently Michael makes this point: He's not forcing anyone to buy his records.

October 16, 1991: Michael with Rick Dees and Chuck Norris at KIIS-FM's celebrity softball game in which the Bolton Bombers took on Dees' Demons. Held at the West Wilshire Park in West Hollywood, the event benefitted the L.A. Regional Food Bank.

And buy them we do! Despite blistering reviews, *Timeless* hit Number One, making Bolton one of just four male solo artists to chart three consecutive Number One albums—the others being Bruce Springsteen, Garth Brooks, and Michael Jackson. Not exactly shabby company, if Bolton needs any consolation.

What the hell is really bugging critics? When he's really aggravated Michael says, "Some just need to be in therapy awhile." As Young pointed out in his *New York Times* profile, plenty of male heavy metal artists sing emotionally but their themes are anger and alienation. He asked: "Why is it more acceptable in 1992 for a singer to sound like he's enraged than to sound like he's weeping?"

It's not as if Bolton violated a code specifying no song shall ever be recorded twice. If there was such a rule his entire career would collapse, sucking much of the music industry into the vortex. Throughout time singers have borrowed one anothers' work. Sometimes the results are wonderful, sometimes dreadful. Sometimes the new version perfectly mimics its forefather, sometimes the song is nearly unrecognizable.

Nowadays cover compilations are a burgeoning genre unto themselves. Consider *Red, Hot, & Blue*, which gathered some unlikely rockers to sing Cole Porter on behalf of AIDS research. *Dedicated* featured new interpretations of Grateful Dead tunes. *Last Temptation of Elvis* gave a diverse crew of singers a crack at Elvis Presley's catalog. *Stay Awake* was an early entry into this market, showcasing rockers singing Disney songs.

In fact, February 16, 1993, marked the release of a combined CD/video titled "For Our Children: The Concert." The show featured artists singing children's songs on behalf of the Pediatric AIDS Foundation. Those who donated their time and talent include Sheila E., Randy Newman, Paula Abdul, spunky rap divas Salt-N-Pepa, Kris Kross, and Michael Bolton crooning "You Are My Sunshine."

Critics accuse Bolton of arrogance. He says, "I've gotten so much bad press for having the gall to record the classics. Like, who do I think I am? But the Beatles, Elvis, the Stones, more recently Phil Collins, a lot of musicians and performers have done it. Anybody has the right to reach into a catalog for a song that meant something to them.

"I think the arrogance is with the person who tells someone else they can't record a certain song. I was really taken aback by this one writer who basically said that there was no reverence for the material I had chosen. This kind of guy I'd just like to take by the shirt and tell him, 'You never contacted me. You never asked me what motivated me to record that song.' It really pisses me off."

One hopes Michael Bolton takes solace in knowing he's not the only popular performer dogged by bad press. Mick Jagger recently said, "I've had so many bad reviews that I wouldn't be able to make another record if I took them seriously. Most of the reviews are written by people who really can't play guitar as well as I can. Or sing at all. Let alone perform. So I don't really have respect for them."

Another blow hit Bolton in the summer of 1992 when the Isley Brothers launched a lawsuit claiming the song he co-wrote with Andrew Goldmark, "Love Is a Wonderful Thing," is a re-worked copy of their 1964 song with the same name, released on UA records and re-issued on an EMI CD in 1991.

The Isleys are suing Bolton in the U.S. District Court in the Central District of California. Ronald Isley claims Michael's song employs the same title, hook, and chorus as his early sixties tune. He might have shrugged it off, but when the Bolton/Goldmark song won awards from both BMI and ASCAP, he saw red.

Isley said, "There's no doubt in my mind that Michael used my song. It's humiliating for Michael to be honored and for the original creators to be ignored. I intend to prosecute my lawsuit vigorously. Someday Michael Bolton will have to return that award. Someday BMI and ASCAP will be giving that award to the Isley Brothers instead."

Louis Levin, Michael's manager, told newspapers, "The song is an original song. We view the claim to be without merit and we are vigorously defending the matter."

Naturally this gave Bolton-bashers cannon fodder. Now it's hip to say he steals left and right. Yet back in 1976 Michael told Ernst Weber he conscientiously reviewed his work to purge it of outside influences. "I really don't want to be refered to as some-one who steals music. . . . I know there are a lot of musicians who think that there's this thing called honor among thieves, and that everybody is ripping off everyone else."

By autumn Bolton was back on an upswing. On October 28, 1992, thousands of fans tuned in for his hour-long NBC-TV special, filmed toward the end of 150 nights on the road with the Time, Love & Tenderness tour. Though Michael joked, "It ain't easy being me," the show, entitled "This Is Michael Bolton," made it seem effortless. Credit must go to the expert production team headed by Bud Schaetzle, who handled Garth Brooks's special aired by the same network earlier that year.

Schaetzle had expected stratospheric ratings for Garth

Brooks, his audience being vast and active. Fishing in the talent pool of pop musicians for his next foray, he decided Michael had the same kind of draw. In the *L.A. Times*, Michael explained, "According to Bud, it was [his] idea that I was one of the only people that—at this time anyway—could pull that kind of audience as well. But I don't know. I'm not taking it for granted, I'll tell you that much. . . . For me it's about a career. It's a way to introduce yourself to a lot of people who, oddly enough, really don't have any idea of who you are."

Originally Bolton hoped to film the special in under a week. Reality proved different as Schaetzle's crew descended on his home, treading into private, personal domain. "It's more in-depth about who I am as a person, my history," said Michael. "It's what it meant to me . . . allowing this dream I have to come true and be greater than I ever meant it to be."

The special was designed to promote his latest album as well as reach out to fans old and new, letting them meet the man behind the sound. It was also a good forum to answer some questions that crop up frequently in Michael's fan mail.

Bolton's team achieved their diverse goals by combining footage from live performances with backstage interviews, film of Bolton's Bombers, Michael's charity softball team, in action on the ball field, Michael at home in Connecticut and in the recording studio with a full orchestra. Affecting tributes came from his mom, Helen; backup singer Vann Johnson; Kenny G; basketball superstar Michael Jordan; and Bolton's frequent producer, Walter Afanasieff. All characterized him as hardworking, tremendously competitive in every endeavor, enormously sincere in all he does.

Bolton's youngest daughters, Holly and Taryn, hover in the background during the Connecticut segments, which Michael considers the most poignant in the show. "The most personal element is when I talk about my kids. [It] takes on a different tone altogether. There's too much to put into this without being a documentary on single fatherhood in the music industry. I could tell that got to the deepest part of me."

While he didn't use the show as a soap box, Michael chose to address some headlines. Explaining why he sings classics, he said, "As a writer you respect a great song, and I think that makes you a better singer, perceiving the subtleties and the important elements of a song. It makes you a better artist. . . . When I want to record a song that's a classic, I want to do it because I love the song. Just to be able to sing a great song by Percy Sledge or Otis Redding or Ray Charles is an enjoyable thing."

Bolton placed enormous stress on his athletic activities. He revisited his childhood Little League field and shot film of Bolton's Bombers playing softball. Michael often claims he relaxes by playing baseball or basketball, though he brings tremendous intensity to these hobbies. When *Esquire*'s Michael Angeli trailed Bolton to Louisiana he found the singer brooding over a softball loss the previous day. Michael hadn't slept for kicking himself over an error that allowed opponents to score twice. He continued berating himself throughout their brunch.

Is this emphasis on butch sportsmanship an attempt to mend fences with men and bring them back into the fold? Ernst Weber, who knew Bolton in the 1970s, doesn't remember him as a jock. Michael says he played a lot of ball during his school days. And he definitely plays now, scheduling games before many tour dates. With a basketball hoop, swimming pool, and home gym at his Connecticut compound, he certainly seems like the real thing.

Bolton insists it's wrong to focus on just one element of his personality, and maybe that's why he's always bringing up sports. "I know what it's been like for me to bump into people who are nothing like what I expected them to be. I was disappointed; then it was harder for me to enjoy their work. I don't want anyone . . . to get that from me. On the other hand, there seems to be a misconception about who I am, especially on the male side. They think I only relate to emotional things."

Concert footage from the special proves that Bolton and his fans have an active mutual admiration society. Every performer, no matter what their metier, finds there's a big difference between live versus filmed or taped performances. The energy level's higher. It's scarier. Bolton agrees there's no substitute for being there. "I'm feeling the audience coming with me and I'm feeding off their excitement and enthusiasm. It creates this kind of momentum. And in that momentum, it hits me as—it's like I'm out in the audience with them and we're all going somewhere together." This excitement and affirmation is the best kind of drug and probably accounts for Bolton's ongoing enthusiasm for touring.

Backup singer Vann Johnson was impressed when Michael advised, "Whatever you sing, you gotta love it!" That, in a nutshell, summarizes his songwriting philosophy. "What you hope you write is a great hit song. . . . The whole industry revolves around hit songs. No matter how big you are, if you come out with an album and it doesn't have hits on it, people don't know you have

an album out. At the same time, you should record songs that
you love. God willing, you're going to perform those songs for a
long, long time."

If it's not easy being Michael Bolton, it's certainly rewarding.
He closed the show by saying: "In so many ways I got a chance
to take this amazing journey. Like everyone else, my life has been
shaped by challenge and disappointment. I learned that when
you trust your instincts and follow your heart, dreams do come
true."

Old and new fans showed their enthusiasm for his special
by making their presence felt in record stores the following week.
Timeless rose to the Number Two slot on the charts; *Time, Love
& Tenderness* went from 59 to 30; and *Soul Provider* climbed from
155 to 75. Recently SMV released an eighty-six-minute video restoring some of the performance and interview footage edited out
of the special.

Even though he's a multi-genre success, Bolton knows he'll
never turn up on the cover of *Rolling Stone*. He's simply not considered cool enough. "[It] would only be attainable for me if I
were to do something very extreme, because I am the antithesis
of the kind of artist they promote. That's a shame, because it's
back to that male problem again."

Never mind. He smiled up from newsstands as *People*'s coverboy for December 7, 1992, touted as a "single father who's got it
all." The interview revealed Bolton at his most introspective, con-
templating fame, romance, and critics. Diane Warren commented, "Michael is a very intense, strong-willed guy and probably the smartest artist I ever met. When you're one-on-one with
him and he's himself, he's hilarious. But sometimes he can be
hardheaded and take things too seriously. Sometimes you want
to go, 'Lighten up, will ya? You're doing great. You're one of the
biggest stars in the world. Enjoy it!'"

It's tough for Michael to let down that protective wall and
even harder for him to chill out. Bolton admits he's a workaholic,
obsessed by his career. That drive has only intensified with success, there's more at stake. "When you finally have what I have,
you don't want anything to jeopardize it," he says. All that's missing is time to relax. "I say, 'My life is screwing up my life.'"

Bolton has no plans to slow down. "I know what it takes to
maintain this. It was a certain kind of focus that got you here and
it is a certain kind of focus that will keep you here. It's like a big
mouth to feed. It's like those old locomotives that you had to keep
shoving coal into otherwise they'd slow down. But it's not about

shoveling coal in, it's a certain type of coal, a creative kind of fuel that you can't allow anybody else to decide about, 'cause it came from you.

"I wanted it. I worked my ass off for it. I *still* work my ass off to keep it and to have it grow, and I'm not gonna be deprived of my enjoyment and pleasure in what I do by some injustice that comes with the picture."

Which brings us back to the critics. But Bolton's got *that* in perspective, too: "Some people can put a lot into a song and there's nowhere else to go. If [critics] listen, they'll see that there's a difference between a B-flat and an E-flat over high C. And I've got that, and I have an F above that if I want it. So I know where I'm taking a song. What they don't get is that I'm taking nine or ten million people with me. Every time out."

(Steve Allen/Gamma Liaison)

8

Success Is a Wonderful Thing

There are unmistakable signs that you've "made it." Being satirized on national television is one indication. Recently Fox network's irreverent comedy "In Living Color" took a crack at Bolton. In the vignette an impersonator decked out in a blond fright wig aped Bolton's dramatic singing style. At the crescendo the singer's head exploded!

Money in the bank is another, sweeter indication. These days Michael Bolton doesn't have to worry about eviction or a steady diet of frozen vegetables. Certainly he's worked hard for the money, but Michael won't admit he's rich. "I've struggled for so long, it's tough for me to find a sense of security."

At long last Bolton can indulge the girls and himself. His modern Connecticut homes are spacious, outfitted with a pool and indoor gym, enlivened by the presence of a frisky black Labrador named Sony. When Bolton loads up his customized bus to embark on a tour, he leaves home and family in the hands of a live-in nanny, a maid, and a cook. If they're in Manhattan, the Boltons can crash at Michael's two-bedroom apartment facing Central Park.

Michael's Westport, Connecticut, home is decorated in shades of cream, white, and fawn. According to *Redbook*'s Pam Lambert, it still doesn't seem fully inhabited, though he's lived there over two years. She found it "spacious, neutral, and neat," almost unnaturally so. *All* of Bolton's homes are strewn with recording paraphernalia so that he can work whenever inspiration strikes. Bolton loves the freedom. "Now I can work all hours like I usually do and still come and have dinner with my kids, which is a new concept in my business."

Like many men Bolton's passionate about cars, and his newfound wealth means good-bye to the shuddering jalopies he drove in the 1970s. His fantasy automobile is a Rolls Royce, 1955 Corniche—cream color! Currently Michael owns a Jeep, a Porsche, and a Mercedes 560 SEL.

When Bolton vacations he prefers zipping off to a hot island to sizzle on the sand. At home he relaxes at the movies. Michael likes everything from Schwarzenegger action films to quieter stories like *Awakenings*. He loved *Dances with Wolves* and enjoys any movie that tells a story about the human spirit.

He also likes to read. His favorite book is *Shibumi* by Trevanian, author of *The Eiger Sanction*. This action thriller, published in 1979, tells the story of Nicholai Hel, the most dangerous man in the world. Hel seeks "shibumi"—a rare kind of personal excellence—and will stop at nothing to achieve it. Bolton's not sure if *he'll* achieve shibumi, but fatalistically says if it's meant to happen it will.

On stage Michael favors expensive, beautifully tailored suits. Off stage he's usually wearing tight black jeans, cowboy boots, and a bright shirt, frequently silk. His favorite color is turquoise. His favorite flowers are white roses.

If the way to a man's heart is through his stomach, women be warned, Michael's favorite foods are Italian pastas, eggplant parmesan, and artichokes. When he orders pizza from Sally's the toppings he prefers are cheese and sun-dried tomatoes. He doesn't have a personal zoo like Michael Jackson, but this Michael has a yen for lions. As for domestic animals, he's partial to German Shepherds.

These and other esoteric facts are traded by members of the Michael Bolton fan club, and another measure of Bolton's success is the enormous attention lavished on its president, Joyce Logan. Bolton's fan club membership has grown enormously, making Joyce a mini-celebrity of the sort that would have warmed Andy Warhol's heart. She's been featured in not one but two *New York Times* articles.

She herself is a diehard fan who writes, "I am so proud of Michael and his deserving fame . . . to watch his career grow to the magnitude that it has is so gratifying to me! He is a wonderful,

106

caring, and sensitive man, and to answer the most asked question, 'Did fame change Michael Bolton?' the answer is, 'Yes, for the better!' . . . I will forever be grateful to call him 'friend.'"

Logan oversees a sophisticated operation from her base in Clinton, Connecticut. Under the aegis of "Fan Emporium" she runs fan clubs for Bolton, Mariah Carey, Wilson Phillips, Kenny G., and Curtis Stigers. A newsletter called *The Bolton Beat* goes out to 8,000 subscribers, and that number rises steadily. Roughly 1,500 letters arrive every week, and Logan screens them all on Michael's behalf.

Joyce is assisted by her cheerful extended family, including her father-in-law (he collects mail), mother-in-law (she sorts it), son (he packs newsletters), and husband (he takes photos for Bolton publications). Other staffers are Judine McGinley, Artist Relations Manager; Kendra Stanley, Barbara Abrams, Susan Kindregan and Dawn Way, Information Exchange Coordinators; Teresa Jackson, Consulting Artist/Illustrator. There's also a foreign pen pal exchange and a collector's exchange. Many members look to the fan club for advance word on tour dates, but Logan cautions that

Michael with Jay Leno, May 14, 1992

(A. Berliner/Gamma Liaison)

107

no schedules can be mailed out until contracts with venues are actually signed.

Those interested in joining (yes, they take credit cards) should contact Fan Emporium, PO Box 679, Branford, CT 06405. For the $18 annual fee new members receive photos, pins, information about merchandise to purchase, quarterly newsletters, fact sheets, and data about Michael's upcoming plans. A portion of the money is donated to This Close for cancer research.

In a memo to new members, Joyce explains, "Your main duty is to be supportive to Michael's career. Call your local radio stations and tell them that you want to hear more of Michael's songs. Write to VH-1 . . . and MTV and encourage them to play his videos." Could all those unsolicited letters to magazine editors be an outgrowth of this concerted epistolary campaign?

What kind of merchandise is available through the fan club? There's a cookbook called *Thyme, Love & Tenderness*, chockful of vegetarian recipes from Michael and his friends (you get an apron with the purchase of five or more books). There are tee shirts and sweatshirts sporting logos and/or photos, an autographed plaque, a Bolton photo mug, tote bags, concert photos, and a calendar. There's even a Michael Bolton racing jacket.

Running Bolton's fan club is exhausting. Joyce spends sixteen hours a day answering letters yet still finds time to tell reporters, "Michael is the only one who gets mail like this. . . . My husband said to slow down . . . I asked him, 'Which letters should I not reply to? This one from the thirteen-year-old girl with brain cancer? This one from an AIDS victim?' "

Logan reckons Michael's appeal is his apparent empathy. "People see him as the perfect husband or brother or family member. They all say, 'You couldn't write a song like that unless you understood this pain.' And they pour out their hearts. . . We get some letters about going to bed with Michael, but more often they're like this one: 'If I could just sit down and have a cup of coffee with him, my life would change.' "

Many people send gifts, which are stored in Logan's offices, so space is a constant problem. Michael prefers donations to his favorite charities over gifts he can't really use or acknowledge. Those charities are:

- This Close, PO Box 3725, New Haven, CT 06525
- National Child Abuse Society, 332 South Michigan Avenue, Suite 1600, Chicago, IL 60604
- Starlight Foundation, 1888 Century Park East, Suite 204, Los Angeles, CA 90067
- Cystic Fibrosis, 6931 Arlington Road, Bethesda, MD 20814

Michael arrives in Los Angeles for the American Music Awards, January 23, 1992.

While it's impossible for Michael to offer himself to everyone who asks, he reaches out when he can. "I get letters from people whose last wish is that I call them. . . . I called a woman with cancer who didn't know if she was going to last through the week. And there was just one second where she said, 'Is this really you?' And I said, 'Yes, it's me.' I Fed-Exed her an autographed letter because I've had the experience of getting mail to someone who was in a coma and didn't come out or calling to find out where to send something and then being told, 'Don't bother sending it, she died.' This has been a gratifying kind of area that I never expected in my life."

A drawback to this extraordinary fame is that Michael is rarely left alone in public. He's not terribly thrilled with that loss of privacy, especially when real fans get pushed aside by thrill-seekers. "One out of five times, some insane girl will grab my hair and stick her nails into my neck because she's snapped. You know, John Kennedy *wanted* to drive with the top down. It's scary. We sometimes do background checks on the fans who write ominous letters.

"Stuff happens now that I could never have imagined. People will do *anything* to get to you . . . people with terrible problems, people with cancer, people whose marriage is falling apart, people who may never see another concert. It makes you very grateful for what you have. So I show up."

Doesn't Michael secretly thrive on all the female attention? Yes and no. What starts out tempting quickly becomes tawdry. "The thing is, women are always available. Beautiful women everywhere. What I can't stand is when they literally throw themselves at you. It's like there's two of me, and they're after the one they think I have no control over—my libido. It's always there, screaming, if you want it."

The ultimate indication that Michael has arrived is his ability to sell tabloids. He's become a headline maker as potent as Elizabeth Taylor, Oprah Winfrey, Princess Diana, or Cher. He jokes, "If I go out to lunch, I can expect a picture everywhere. If I do business with a woman, it could show up all over the world. It comes with the territory; you shrug it off."

Bolton's love life gets a lot of ink, especially now that he dates an equally high-profile companion, actress Nicollette Sheridan. He'd prefer to stay silent, but that's a virtually impossible option. Even as he complains, "My personal life is one of the last hold-outs people can't get access to," Michael fields the inevitable questions gracefully.

109   Nicollette became a tabloid regular when her private life took on the complexity of a plotline from her show "Knots Landing." She and former "L.A. Law" actor Harry Hamlin starred in a made-for-cable movie together, then continued their onscreen romance offscreen, to the great displeasure of Hamlin's wife, who kicked him out. He moved in with Sheridan and soon asked her to be his newest bride. Wedding preparations occupied gossips for months with enormous attention paid to the minutiae of rivaling-for-bad-taste his-and-hers bachelor parties. The tabloids seemed pretty disappointed when the wedding actually occurred.

They weren't down for long. Within months Nicollette and Harry separated. Soon Nicollette, who's about ten years Michael's junior, turned up on Bolton's arm. They're old acquaintances who met years earlier through Kenny G.

Michael admitted he was "nervous about exposing myself emotionally. When she moved out I felt more comfortable spending time with her, getting to know her. Even then, the little kid in me would say, 'Is she gonna go running back? Are they really over?'" Ever the concerned mother, Helen Bolotin wondered, "Couldn't you find someone who isn't married?"

By fall, Michael and Nicollette were secure enough about their feelings to go public. In October they were photographed at Hollywood's Carousel of Hope Ball. Michael also introduced Nicollette to his family that autumn, and the beautiful blond won rave reviews. Of course, Bolton expected a harmonious encounter. "I wouldn't be attracted to a woman who wouldn't understand how important my kids are to me. And Nicollette is perfect that way."

Taryn, his youngest, is especially pleased with Nicollette. Bolton says they have "great rapport." Isa and Holly? "I know there's respect with the other girls, but along with that I think there's more of that awareness than an older teenager has. But I haven't seen the kind of trauma—or drama—that will ruin a good time."

Bolton's friend and collaborator Diane Warren gives the match high marks. "Nicollette is intelligent. She's not a bimbo. She doesn't put up with his crap. When you're in his position, everyone's telling you what you want to hear. She's honest. She's not a passive yes-woman."

Michael claims he was initially attracted by Nicollette's great looks, but her terrific personality keeps him enraptured. "Nicollette is incredible. She's a beautiful, strong woman who isn't afraid to speak her mind." Because Michael believes "deep communication makes it work," he needs someone who's not just a lover or an ornament, but a best friend, too. He's partial to women who are bright and sweet and blessed with a sense of humor, security, and a strong urge for privacy.

Will Michael and Nicollette marry? Sensibly, Bolton denies it for now. Ordinarily he wouldn't comment on rumors, but fans were sending presents. "People write things about you and there's no telling where they got it from. I've been getting fan mail like crazy from people [who] want to know where to send the wedding gifts. I said, 'Tell them there's no wedding. And tell them not to believe what they read, especially in the tabloids.' "

According to those tabloids, Sheridan enthused to a friend, "Michael has everything I've ever wanted—good looks, a great career, sensitivity and passion. It may have taken time to find the right man, but Michael is definitely the last stop for me." The papers alleged the duo toured Los Angeles jewelry stores searching for a perfect engagement ring, something tasteful and unique.

Bolton's not terribly worried about Nicollette's reaction to rumors, partly because she's a celebrity herself and partly because communication is the foundation of their match. "If you have a great relationship with someone—and to me, there's no point in having [one] unless it's going to be a great one—there's a certain amount of consideration that has to be taken, so no one reads something or hears something that maybe you could have warned each other about. I want to be able to be open about everything."

One rumor, however, brings up an especially hot topic: Michael's hair. Michael Bolton's hair is a national preoccupation. Fans adore it, but for everyone who fantasizes about running her fingers through those locks, someone else asks, "What *is* it with that hair?"

According to one tabloid, Nicollette gave Michael an ultimatum: the hair or me! Coming mere weeks after a banner promising "Michael Bolton to Wed," the new story had them on the verge of a breakup. It said Sheridan objected to Michael's vast collection of haircare products and extensive grooming time (including fifty brushstrokes both day and night). The final straw came when Nicollette caught her gold bracelet in his tresses during a tender moment. An unnamed source told *The Star*, "Nic thinks Michael would look sexy with a short buzz. . . . She tells him long hair and pony tails are out for men."

Despite jokes about hair extensions, Michael has worn his hair long forever. Photos from the early days show it tumbling down his back, and Helen talks about going up against school officials over Michael's pony tail.

People are buzzing about the fact that Michael's hair is si-

Michael does his thing with the Bolton Bombers.

All photos Mark Ridings

multaneously long and short, and noticeably wispy on top. The long portions look distressed where they used to be full and wavy. The cover of *Soul Provider* gives the first hint that his top layer is thinning. By the time Columbia released *Timeless*, art directors hit on a clever diversion: they printed Michael's name over his receding hairline. Has overly zealous grooming taken its toll? Or is it simply age? Writer Michael Angeli compared Bolton's coif to the "grandmother's wig Tony Perkins wore in *Psycho*." Many echo that sentiment, referring to it as steel wool frizz.

Should it stay or go? *Star* polled readers, aiding their imaginations with a "computer generated" photo of Bolton in short hair. It's a wonder they bothered; it doesn't require an enormous leap to imagine this. When votes were tallied, fully 82 percent urged Bolton to keep his hair long, 16 percent said cut it off, and 2 percent couldn't decide.

A Nova Scotia reader opined: "If Michael cuts his hair, it would be the same as Samson snipping his for Delilah. No way! It's very much a part of his sexy image."

Another reader wrote: "Heck, with the jewelry in it, Michael's hair becomes even more precious." Several advised Nicollette to strip down before clutching her beau, and a few offered to date him in her place.

On the snip side, a voter from Michigan complained: "Michael's hair is too thin to wear long. It looks straggly and unkempt." One Texan compared it to "a rat's nest." Finally, a Hollywood reader decided the point was moot: "Michael will still be unattractive to me regardless of what he does with his hair."

Sensibly, Bolton himself steered well clear of the great hair debate. With the pressures of an international tour, parenthood, and a new album to contemplate, he hardly had time. And when Bolton *does* have a free moment he rarely loafs but maintains an extraordinarily active schedule of charitable activities that would stagger professional philanthropists.

Michael Bolton is quite dedicated to helping friends, family, and those less fortunate than himself. Mindful of his own early hardships, Michael is not content to build an ivory tower, fill the moat, and raise the drawbridge. Instead, he compassionately gives of himself throughout the year making personal appearances, playing sports, performing benefits, and taping public service announcements.

"I think of how fortunate I've been and I've worked all my life to get here. Nobody handed me anything. So many people are so successful from what this country has to offer, it's not such a big deal to give it back. It's not gonna change the way you live."

For Michael, actions speak louder than words. He's not inspired to write controversial, cause-oriented songs. "I don't really think that does anything. I think you have a hit and then it goes away and the problem's still there. It's about directing your energy into areas that focus on this kind of thing, including television, documentaries."

So don't expect Bolton to shock his fans like some of rock's more overtly political performers. He's utterly disinterested in Madonna's sexual campaign but does admire Ice-T, though not his single "Cop Killer." "Every impression I have of Ice-T is that he's a very intelligent, sensitive, and intense kind of person. I like him, so I was a little surprised at this whole thing. He wants to involve himself in important issues, which is something that I kind of want to do a bit more of myself. There's a lot of healing that needs to be done."

Bolton returned to this theme during his TV special: "Something that I never really expected . . . [is] the healing power, the healing aspect of music. I get a lot of mail from all kinds of people having some really tough times, telling me how much my music helps."

Since 1991, Bolton has been an active volunteer for the National Committee to Prevent Child Abuse (NCPCA). Joy Byers, an NCPCA spokesperson, says Bolton approached the group asking how he could help. His first project was a thirty-second public service announcement distributed by the Ad Council of New York to radio stations nationwide. That announcement generated terrific response, and Byers still receives mail from fans inspired to seek parenting information.

Next, Target stores and Coca-Cola joined forces and donated a percentage of their sales to NCPCA. Bolton created a new public service announcement, filmed this time, to run over the winter holidays. It featured him surrounded by children in a festive Christmas setting.

Bolton's devotion to NCPCA is so unstinting he received a special honor from former First Lady Barbara Bush for his efforts. He told the North Carolina *News & Observer*, "As far as a personal interest in the prevention of child abuse, well, I have three girls. I've read about child abuse. . . . [It's] the most unthinkable, appalling thing. Nobody even wants to imagine it. But when you hear the statistics and you learn how common it is, you've just got to do something about it."

In fact, Bolton's so sympathetic to kids that he went ballistic when female fans at a Louisiana concert waved their babies in the air like banners to get his attention. Outraged, he told an employee: "The baby-waving's gotta stop. The kids don't know me from Big Bird. It's dangerous, and on top of it, it's disgusting. It's usury. . . . One woman let go of her kid, and I thought she would break his jaw. I wanted to take the mother and slam her. I suppose that could be bad press."

Joy Byers is pleased to have someone as visible as Michael Bolton championing the NCPCA. "He cares a great deal about this issue. He's actually gotten involved and he's willing to use his time and energy. We're very grateful for that. Sometimes it takes a person like Michael Bolton, who people can relate to, to get the message across. People like the idea that someone they like has gotten involved in something they believe in."

Though it's not encouraged, fans occasionally write to Bolton in care of the NCPCA. Byers says she keeps him posted on how the letters are answered. "He was shocked by the first batch. Michael said, 'I had no idea that people would respond like that and open up about their problems like that.'"

Joy is a fan of the man, not just the celebrity. "I love being around him and talking to him. He's a real person who truly cares. There's nothing phony about him."

Michael also raises money for This Close, a group started by a childhood friend Joel Brander, who developed leukemia. This Close sponsors research into potential cancer cures. Bolton's two benefit concerts raised hundreds of thousands of dollars for the charity. He also donates a portion of the proceeds from his fan club to This Close.

On January 16, 1993, Bolton sang at a benefit held in Manhattan's Paramount Theater to generate donations for City Kids, which aids underprivileged urban youths. The next day Bolton hopped a plane for Florida and a charity softball game on behalf of Habitat for Humanity. That money was routed into assistance for Dade County, still rebuilding after a devastating hurricane. At the game he met idol Joe DiMaggio, who Bolton calls "one of the nicest people I've met and a classy guy." As DiMaggio reminisced about his baseball career, Michael couldn't help thinking of his dad—a diehard Yankee fan—and how thrilled he'd have been by their meeting.

Bolton's busiest ongoing charity association is the softball team Bolton's Bombers (formerly Bolton's Bad Boys), whose record for the summer of 1992 was 17 and 3. The team is composed of musicians, record company executives, and members of Bolton's entourage. In 1992 that included Dennis Rodriguez, Mugs Cain, Louis Levin, Joey Melotti, Pat McCollum, Gary Reynolds, Steve Crandall, Kevin Tyler, Chris Camozzi, and Schuyler Deale.

116

(John Paschal/Celebrity Photo)

Michael with Mariah
Carey at the
Nineteenth Annual
American Music
Awards at the Shrine
Auditorium in Los
Angeles on January
27, 1992. He won for
Favorite Male Artist
in Pop/Rock; she
won for Favorite
Female Artist in
Soul/Rhythm &
Blues.

The Bombers play before concerts to generate money for lo-cal charities in cities along their tour route. Their first game of the '92 season raised $13,000 for the Milwaukee Hunger Task Force; their final game brought hundreds of canned goods for the Richmond, Virginia Children's Hospital. A softball game in Ra-leigh, North Carolina, raised $3,000 for the local chapter of NCPCA. Other games raised cash for United Cerebral Palsy, the Ronald McDonald House in Memphis, and "Just Say No" Foun-dation in Lafayette, Louisiana.

Michael says playing ball is a pleasure, not a chore. "On the road I was doing softball games between every show and you realize . . . you did twenty fund-raisers while having the time of your life—what is the catch? For me, I feel a sense of responsibil-ity to help other people in less fortunate situations."

On February 8, 1993, Bolton turned up in person to donate $50,000 to the Harlem School of the Arts, located at 645 St. Nich-olas Avenue in New York City. The twenty-nine-year-old school,

run by executive/artistic director Darryl Durham, plans to utilize this money—half from Michael, half from his record company—to establish scholarships, create performance opportunities, and offer financial aid to students. Some of this donation comes from the Michael Bolton Foundation, which was partially funded by proceeds from sales of *Timeless*.

Addressing a group of Manhattan politicians, teachers, and students, Bolton explained, "This is just one of the appropriate ways that I can think of to show the obvious and tremendous contribution that African-Americans have made to our culture and my career." Months earlier he told the *New York Times*, "The idea is to give scholarships so black children have the opportunity to pursue their gift. I want to give something back."

Then on March 9, 1993, Bolton headlined a benefit held at the dance club The Ritz, in New York City, to raise money for Forward Face, which sponsors reconstructive surgery for disfiguring birth defects.

With a schedule this busy, it's a wonder Bolton has any time left to pursue his career.

(Barry King/Gamma Liaison)

9

From Now On

If 1992 got off to a rocky start, 1993 began *splendidly*, suggesting this should be a powerhouse decade for the nation's most popular balladeer. Fans thronged to a New Year's Eve celebration at Madison Square Garden marking Michael's first area appearance in more than a year. Though costly—$75, $50, and $27.50—tickets sold out instantly.

In January, Michael journeyed to Washington, D.C., to welcome Bill Clinton to the White House. He participated in the star-studded American Reunion, which mixed and matched such celebrities as Barbra Streisand, Warren Beatty, Annette Bening, Aretha Franklin, Diana Ross, Michael Jackson, Stevie Wonder, Jack Nicholson, Jack Lemmon, Chuck Berry, Tony Bennett, and L. L. Cool J. Bolton's father, who dedicated his life to the party, would have been proud to know his son's participation was personally solicited by the country's first Democratic president in more than a decade. And prouder still if he'd been alive to see Michael take the stage before the Lincoln Memorial and wow the inaugural celebrants with a show-stopping rendition of "Lean on Me" that even inspired a spontaneous round of applause from the backup choir.

Bolton joined Clinton's bandwagon at a Chicago rally. His appearance drew a huge crowd, and Clinton's people immediately recognized a valuable ally. The candidate personally telephoned Bolton to ask if he'd attend a subsequent rally planned for New Jersey. Michael remembers, "He called me . . . which was quite a thrill. . . . When I spoke to Bill—he told me to call him Bill—I just got such a good feeling from him. I've been around politicians since I was very young, and I've always felt that they were aggressive, ambitious people."

At the inauguration someone approached Bolton to say, "Ray would like to see you." This, it turned out, meant Ray Charles. Michael was scared. "Okay, did I do something? It was like going to the principal's office." They chatted for about twenty minutes about music and singing. Then Ray startled Michael by asking for some songs. "I'm going through my whole catalog thinking, what do I have for Ray? I'd love to have Ray Charles do one of my songs."

On January 25, Bolton escorted Nicollette Sheridan to the Twentieth American Music Awards, hosted by the unlikely triumvirate Bobby Brown, Wynonna Judd, and Gloria Estefan. Decked out in a dark suit and shirt, Bolton sang a medley of "To Love Somebody" and "Drift Away." He collected awards for Best Adult Contemporary Artist and Best Male Pop/Rock Artist. There were no Grammy nominations in 1993 and he didn't attend the ceremonies. Who can blame him?

March marked the release of *Michael Bolton: Soul & Passion*, a 12-track, 55-minute video compilation featuring most of Michael's best-loved songs. Here are the three previously released videos, "How Am I Supposed to Live Without You," "Soul Provider," and "How Can We Be Lovers," plus nine more tracks. When you see Michael actually perform his songs, even amidst the contrivances of a video, they carry even more emotional weight than they do on CD. Somehow the simplicity of their lyrics melts away and it's apparent just how effective he is at putting a song across.

"That's What Love Is All About" is a concept video composed of vignettes showing Michael alternately enjoying a woman's company or gazing at her from afar. "Dock of the Bay" takes place on the most pristine wharf ever created by an art director, populated by model-quality "forgotten men" who turn out to be musicians. For "Wait on Love" Bolton conjures a club setting full of Lycra-clad cuties grooving to his performance. It was clever of Bolton to make this a straightforward, unpretentious video, since the song is not as strong as many of his other hits.

The classy black and white video for "Georgia on My Mind" recreates a basement blues club. Michael and Kenny G join a jazz

At the Presidential Inauguration, 1993

(Cynthia Johnson/Gamma Liaison)

combo to deliver this nostalgic hit. "When I'm Back on My Feet Again" effectively alternates color with black and white shots, performance with concept. For the former, Michael's placed in a dramatically lit warehouse. This is mixed with clips of people facing troubles: a wheelchair-bound man lifting weights, Michael dressed as an old man hobbling along with a cane, and a woman coping with alcohol addiction.

By contrast, the very up-tempo song "Love Is a Wonderful Thing" fairly bursts with color, energy, and cleavage. Again Bolton mixes performance with concept, depicting a series of couples acting goofy in the name of love. "Time, Love & Tenderness" is a behind-the-scenes recreation of a recording session. The artist at work is also the theme of "Steel Bars" a definitive rock star clip video showing Bolton backstage, on a tour bus, at the sound check, and finally, performing for a packed stadium.

For "Missing You Now" Bolton enacts a fully evolved love story. When his car breaks down, it's towed to a service station run by an older mechanic and his beautiful daughter. While Dad toils under the hood, Bolton bonds with the lady. But alas, his job takes him away again. Their romantic phone calls and exuberant reunion round out the sensual clip.

Though he'll be playing dates in Europe during late spring, winter 1993 finds Bolton absorbed in his new album. Typically he starts work late in the day and stays up later, often until dawn. It takes about three and a half months to record an album, not including his writing time. Toward the end, Michael puts in about

121

At a benefit for New York City's needy kids, with Roger Daltrey, January 16, 1993

(Allen/Gamma Liaison)

At the American Music Awards, 1992

(Vinnie Zuffante/Star File)

Bill Thorup/X-Press Studio

With Luther Vandross at the American Music Awards, 1992

(Vinnie Zuffante/Star File)

(Barry King/Gamma Liaison)

thirty solid fourteen- to sixteen-hour days. He's a perfectionist (some say prima donna) who must approve every detail from Christmas ribbons to publicity stills. At photo sessions he insists a full-length mirror be placed alongside the *photographer* during photo shoots so that he can constantly keep tabs on the progress. It's not surprising that he fights to get each album cut sounding its best.

What will be on the new album? That's a carefully guarded secret. Smart money's on ballads, ballads, and more ballads. But Michael's not in a rush. With success comes bigger album budgets. Bolton's luxuriating in the freedom to indulge his perfectionism. "It's not about the money. The most important thing is making the best record of your life. Every time you make a record."

Fans will undoubtedly be pleased with the outcome. As Michael joked, "I'm not about to take a sudden left turn and decide I'm going to do my 'Free the Baby Whales Off the Coast of South America' record." Still, his album won't be without ecological impact. Columbia is one of several labels switching to Eco-Pak, a streamlined CD package relying on fold-out cardboard panels instead of a hard plastic box. That requires less plastic and cardboard so there's little waste—only the shrink wrap is thrown away.

In 1993 Bolton also became one of the first performers to join the Alliance of Artists and Recording Companies, created under the auspices of the Recording Industry Association of America (RIAA) to collect artist digital home taping royalties. Other charter members include Whitney Houston, Tom Petty, and Stevie Nicks.

In addition to his thriving musical career, Bolton belongs to the ranks of singers who plan to pursue acting. He made at least one reconnaissance mission to Hollywood and was shocked to discover the movie community is even more cutthroat than New York's fast-paced recording industry! "I'm used to being with people in radio. TV and movie people are different. 'Front' is a lot more important to them. The real Hollywood guy is always smiling, no matter what. Everybody's hugging with knives in their hands. In New York you see the knife. In the music business you generally know where you stand."

Even if he succumbs to the lure of greasepaint, Michael won't head west permanently, though he spends lots of time there. His roots run too deep. "I've never really been able to get that far away from Connecticut," he admits. "There's always something that brings me back here. And never too far away from New Haven, the city of my birth. There's something about the way of life here and

Best Wishes

the pace of things that's just right. This is really where I want to raise my kids."

For the first time ever Michael Bolton has both the writing and singing portions of his career going full blast, so don't ask him to pick one or the other exclusively. "It's impossible to choose. Left side or right side of your body—which would you function with?" Clearly Bolton knows the value of balance.

After struggling so hard and so long without recognition, Michael's amazed that his dream is a reality. "It just keeps coming true, everything you've worked for is happening. And everything—as a child—you wanted, is finally taking place. I have to say there's never been a question in my mind or in my heart what I was meant to do, since I was a kid. Before I had my first serious relationship, before I was married, long before I had children, there was a love for music."

He has no regrets. "Even if I had had success doing that arena-rock thing, it would probably have been over by now. What I'm doing now promises much more longevity, and I love doing it." It's true, then, that things we work hardest for offer the sweetest rewards.

Basically Michael's doing the job he really wants to do and that makes him an incredibly lucky fellow. "I'm just glad . . . [I] do what I love to do for a living while 99 percent of the people I know in the world can't. On top of it, I make people feel good. I think I can deal with that."

His career is a testimony to hard work, patience, and faith. "I'm still learning a lot about myself. But I've found that when you reach, really reach, and set your sights beyond what's attainable, you're amazed at what can happen. . . . I never really studied music. It swept me away! Music is the air I breathe, how I express myself. I want to move women to tears—and men—with my vocal ability and strength."

Index